ASTRONOMY WITH REALITY

SANDEEP BISHT

Made with ♥ on the Notion Press Platform
www.notionpress.com

Astronomy With Reality

By- Sandeep Bisht

Contents

PREFACE

Content

Prologue

I

THE SHAPE OF THE EARTH

Astronomical Problems respecting the Earth.—The earth is one of the objects belonging to the field of astronomical investigations. In the consideration of it astronomy has its closest contact with some of the other sciences, particularly with geology and meteorology. Those problems respecting the earth that can be solved for other planets also, or that are essential for the investigation of other astronomical questions, are properly considered as belonging to the field of astronomy.

The astronomical problems respecting the earth can be divided into two general classes. The first class consists of those which can be treated, at least to a large extent, without regarding the earth as a member of a family of planets or considering its relations to them and the sun. Such problems are its shape and size, its mass, its density, its interior temperature and rigidity, and the constitution, mass, height, and effects of its atmosphere. These problems will be treated in this chapter. The second class consists of the problems involved in the relations of the earth to other bodies, particularly its rotation, revolution around the sun, and the consequences of these motions. The treatment of these problems will be reserved for the next chapter. It would be an easy matter simply to state the astronomical facts respecting the earth, but in science it is necessary not only to say what things are true but also to give the reasons for believing that they are true.

Therefore one or more proofs will be given for the conclusions astronomers have reached respecting the earth. As a matter of logic one complete proof is sufficient, but it must be remembered that a scientific doctrine consists of, and rests on, a great number of theories whose truth may be more or less in question, and consequently a number of proofs is always desirable. If they agree, their agreement confirms belief in the accuracy of all of them. It will not be regarded as a burden to follow carefully these proofs; in fact, one who has arrived at a mature stage of intellectual development instinctively demands the reasons we have for believing that our conclusions are sound.

The Simplest and most Conclusive Proof of the Earth's Sphericity—Among the proofs that the earth is found, the simplest and most conclusive is that the plane of the horizon, or the direction of the plumb line, changes by an angle which is directly proportional to the distance the observer travels along the surface of the earth, whatever the direction and distance of travel.

It will be shown first that if the earth were a true sphere the statement would be true. For simplicity, suppose the observer travels along a meridian. If the statement is true for this case, it will be true for all others, because a sphere has the same curvature in every direction. Suppose the observer starts from O1, Fig., and travels northward to O2. The length of the arc O1O2 is proportional to the angle a which it subtends at the center of the sphere.

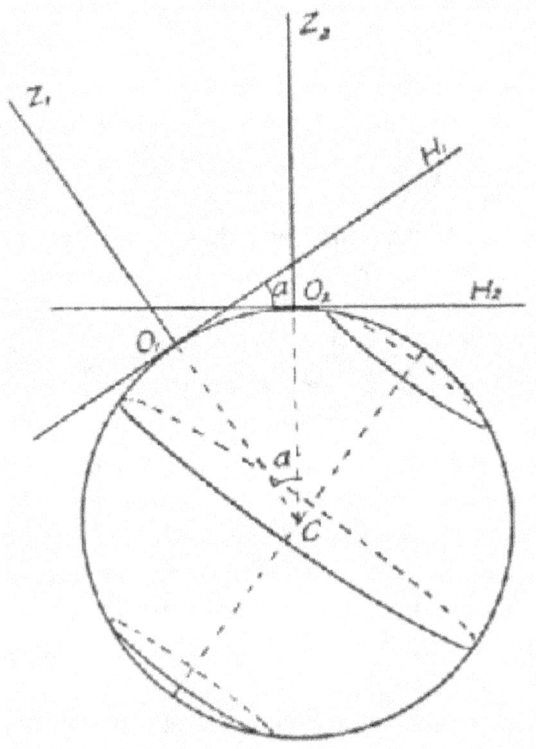

The change in the direction of the plumb line is proportional to the distance traveled along the surface of the earth.

The planes of the horizon of O1 and O2 are respectively O1H1 and O2H2. These lines are respectively perpendicular to CO1 and CO2. Therefore the angle between them equals the angle a. That is, the distance traveled is proportional to the change of direction of the plane of the horizon. The plumb lines at O1 and O2 are respectively O1Z1 and O2Z2, and the angle between these lines is a. Hence the distance traveled is proportional to the change in the direction of the plumb line.

It will be shown now that if the surface of the earth were not a true sphere the change in the direction of the plane of the horizon would not be proportional to the distance traveled on the surface. Suppose Fig. represents a plane section through the non-spherical earth along whose surface the observer travels. Since the earth is not a sphere, the curvature of its surface will be different at different places. Suppose that O_1O_2 is one of the flatter regions and O_3O_4 is one of the more convex ones. In the neighborhood of O_1O_2 the direction of the plumb line changes slowly, while in the neighborhood of O_3O_4 its direction changes more rapidly.

The large arc O_1O_2 subtends an angle at C_1 made by the respective perpendiculars to the surface which exactly equals the angle at C_3 subtended by the smaller arc O_3O_4. Therefore in this case the change in direction of the plumb line is not proportional to the distance traveled, for the same angular change corresponds to two different distances. The same result is true for the plane of the horizon because it is always perpendicular to the plumb line.

Since the conditions of the statement would be satisfied in case the earth were spherical, and only in case it were spherical, the next question is what the observations show. Except for irregularities of the surface, which are not under consideration here, and the oblateness, which will be discussed in Art. 12, the observations prove absolutely that the change in direction of the plumb line is proportional to the arc traversed.

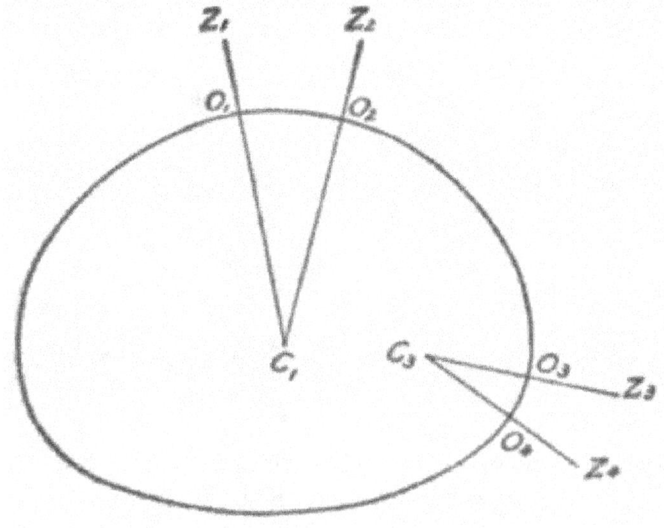

If the earth were not spherical, equal angles would be subtended
by arcs of different lengths.

Two practical problems are involved in carrying out the proof
which has just been described. The first is that of measuring the
distance between two points along the surface of the earth, and the
second is that of determining the change in the direction of the
plumb line. The first is a refined problem of surveying; the second is
solved by observations of the stars.

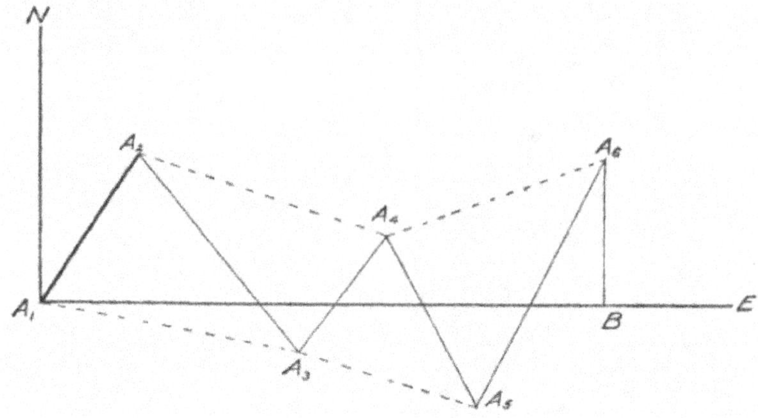

The base line A1A2 is measured directly and the other distances are obtained by triangulation.

All long distances on the surface of the earth are determined by a process known as triangulation. It is much more convenient than direct measurement and also much more accurate. A fairly level stretch of country, A1 and A2 in Fig. , a few miles long is selected, and the distance between the two points, which must be visible from each other, is measured with the greatest possible accuracy. This line is called the base line. Then a point A3 is taken which can be seen from both A1 and A2. A telescope is set up at A1 and pointed at A2. It has a circle parallel to the surface of the earth on which the degrees are marked. The position of the telescope with respect to this circle is recorded. Then the telescope is turned until it points toward A3. The difference of its position with respect to the circle when pointed at A2 and at A3 is the angle A2A1A3. Similarly, the telescope is set up at A2 and the angle A1A2A3 is measured.

Then in the triangle A1A2A3 two angles and the included side are known. By plane geometry, two triangles that have two angles and the included side of one respectively equal to two angles and the included side of the other are exactly alike in size and shape. This simply means that when two angles and the included side of the triangle are given, the triangle is uniquely defined. The remaining parts can be computed by trigonometry. In the present case suppose the distance A2A3 is computed.

Now suppose a fourth point A4 is taken so that it is visible from both A2 and A3. Then, after the angles at A2 and A3 in the triangle A2A3A4 have been measured, the line A3A4 can be computed. This process evidently can be continued, step by step, to any desired distance. Suppose A1 is regarded as the original point from which measurements are to be made. Not only have various distances been determined, but also their directions with respect to the north-south line are known. Consequently, it is known how far north and how far east A2 is from A1.

The next step gives how far south and how far east A3 is from A2. By combining the two results it is known how far south and how far east A3 is from A1, and so on for succeeding points. The convenience in triangulation results partly from the long distances that can be measured, especially in rough country. It is sometimes advisable to go to the trouble of erecting towers in order to make it possible to use stations separated by long distances. The accuracy arises, at least in part, from the fact that the angles are measured by instruments which magnify them.

The fact that the stations are not all on the same level, and the curvature of the earth, introduce little difficulties in the computations that must be carefully overcome. The direction of the plumb line at the station A1, for example, is determined by noting the point among the stars at which it points. The plumb line at A2 will point to a different place among the stars. The difference in the two places among the stars gives the difference in the directions of the plumb lines at the two stations. The stars apparently move across the sky from east to west during the night and are not in the same positions at the same time of the day on different nights. Hence, there are here also certain circumstances to which careful attention must be given in order to get accurate results.

Other Proofs of the Earth's Sphericity.—

There are many reasons given for believing that the earth is not a plane, and that it is, indeed, some sort of a convex figure; but most of them do not prove that it is actually spherical. It will be sufficient to mention them.

(a) The earth has been circumnavigated, but so far as this fact alone is concerned it might be the shape of a cucumber.

(b) Vessels disappear below the horizon hulls first and masts last, but this only proves the convexity of the surface.

(c) The horizon appears to be a circle when viewed from an elevation above the surface of the water. This is theoretically good but observationally it is not very exact.

(d) The shadow of the earth on the moon at the time of a lunar eclipse is always an arc of a circle, but this proof is very inconclusive, in spite of the fact that it is often mentioned, because the shadow has no very definite edge and its radius is large compared to that of the moon.

Proof of the Oblateness of the Earth by Arcs of Latitude.—

The latitude of a place on the earth is determined by observations of the direction of the plumb line with respect to the stars. This is the reason that a sea captain refers to the heavenly bodies in order to find his location on the ocean. It is found by actual observations of the stars and measurements of arcs that the length of a degree of arc is longer the farther it is from the earth's equator. the earth is less curved at the poles than it is at the equator. A body which is thus flattened at the poles and bulged at the equator is called oblate.

In order to see that in the case of an oblate body a degree of latitude is longer near the poles than it is at the equator, consider Fig. In this figure E represents a plane section of the body through its poles. The curvature at the equator is the same as the curvature of the circle C1, and a degree of latitude on E at its equator equals a degree of latitude on C1. The curvature of E at its pole is the same as the curvature of the circle C2, and a degree of latitude on E at its pole equals a degree of latitude on C2. Since C2 is greater than C1, a degree of latitude near the pole of the oblate body is greater than a degree of latitude near its equator.

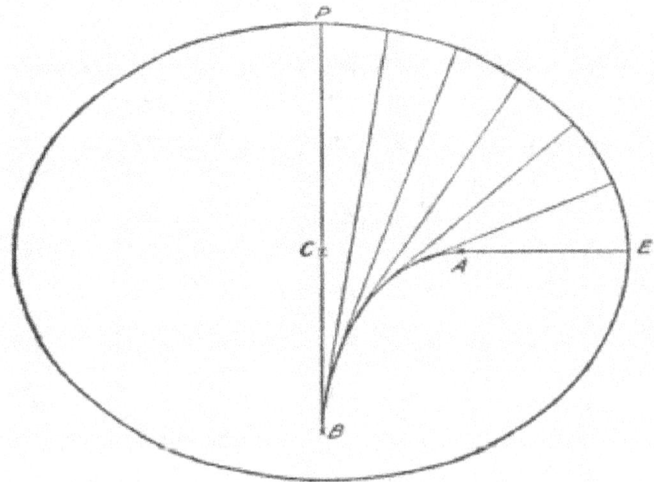

Perpendiculars to the surface of an oblate body, showing that equal arcs subtend largest angles at its equator and smallest at its poles.

A false argument is sometimes made which leads to the opposite conclusion. Lines are drawn from the center of the oblate body dividing the quadrant into a number of equal angles. Then it is observed that the arc intercepted between the two lines nearest the equator is longer than that intercepted between the two lines nearest the pole. The error of this argument lies in the fact that, with the exception of those drawn to the equator and poles, these lines are not perpendicular to the surface. Figure shows an oblate body with a number of lines drawn perpendicular to its surface. Instead of their all passing through the center of the body, they are tangent to the curve AB. The line AE equals the radius of a circle having the same curvature as the oblate body at E, and BP is the radius of the circle having the curvature at P.

The dimensions of the earth have been computed with great accuracy by Hayford, who found for the equatorial diameter 7926.57 miles, and for the polar diameter 7899.98 miles. The error in these results cannot exceed a thousand feet. The equatorial circumference is 24, 901.7 miles, and the length of one degree of longitude at the equator is 69.17 miles. The lengths of degrees of latitude at the equator and at the poles are respectively 69.40 and 68.71 miles. The total area of the earth is about 196, 400, 000 square miles. The volume of the earth is equal to the volume of a sphere whose radius is 3958.9 miles.

Newton's Proof of the Oblateness of the Earth.—

The first proof that the earth is oblate was due to Newton. He based his demonstration on the laws of motion, the law of gravitation, and the rotation of the earth. It is therefore much more complicated than that depending on the lengths of degrees of latitude, which is purely geometrical. It has the advantage, however, of not requiring any measurements of arcs.

Imagine that a tube filled with water exists reaching from the pole P to the center C, and then to the surface on the equator at Q. The water in this tube exerts a pressure toward the center because of the attraction of the earth for it. Consider a unit volume in the part CP at any distance D from the center; the pressure it exerts toward the center equals the earth's attraction for it because it is subject to no other forces. Suppose for the moment that the earth is a sphere, as it would be if it were not rotating on its axis, and consider a unit volume in the part CQ at the distance D from the center.

Because of the symmetry of the sphere it will be subject to an attraction equal to that on the corresponding unit in CP. But, in addition to the earth's attraction, this mass of water is subject to the centrifugal force due to the earth's rotation, which to some extent counter-balances the attraction. Therefore, the pressure it exerts toward the center is less than that exerted by the corresponding unit in CP. If the earth were spherical, all units in the two columns could be paired in this way. The result would be that the pressure exerted by P C would be greater than that exerted by QC; but such a condition would not be one of equilibrium, and water would flow out of the mouth of the tube from the center to the equator.

In order that the two columns of water shall be in equilibrium the equatorial column must be longer than the polar. Newton computed the amount RQ by which the one tube must be longer than the other in order that for a body having the mass, dimensions, and rate of rotation of the earth, there should be equilibrium. This gave him the oblateness of the earth. In spite of the fact that his data were not very exact, he obtained results which agree very well with those furnished by modern measurements of arcs.

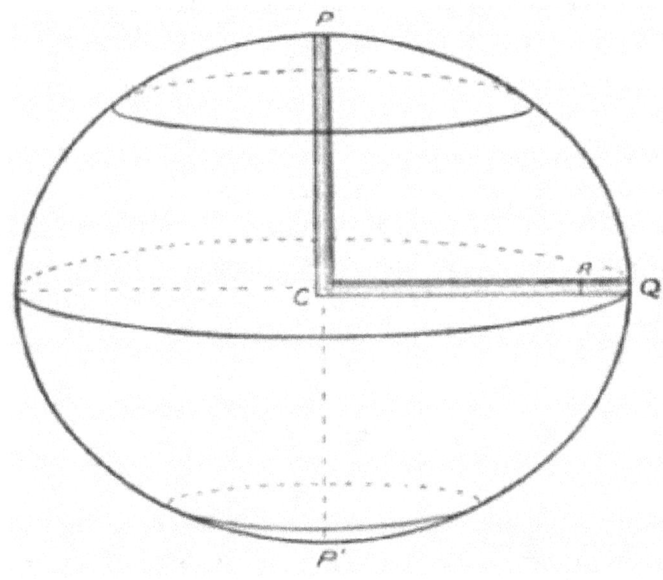

Because of the earth's rotation around P P0 the column CQ must be longer than P C.

The objection at once arises that the tubes did not actually exist and that they could not possibly be constructed, and therefore that the conclusion was as insecure as those usually are which rest on imaginary conditions. But the fears aroused by these objections are dissipated by a little more consideration of the subject. It is not necessary that the tubes should run in straight lines from the surface to the center in order that the principle should apply. They might bend in any manner and the results would be the same, just as the level to which the water rises in the spout of a teakettle does not depend on its shape. Suppose the tubes are deformed into a single one connecting P and Q along the surface of the earth. The principles still hold; but the ocean connection of pole and equator may be considered as being a tube. Hence the earth must be oblate or the ocean would flow from the poles toward the equator.

Pendulum Proof of the Oblateness of the Earth.—

It seems strange at first that the shape of the earth can be determined by means of the pendulum. Evidently the method cannot rest on such simple geometrical principles as were sufficient in using the lengths of arcs. It will be found that it involves the laws of motion and the law of gravitation.

The time of oscillation of a pendulum depends on the intensity of the force acting on the bob and on the distance from the point of support to the bob. It is shown in analytic mechanics that the formula for a complete oscillation is

$$t = 2\pi \sqrt{l/g},$$

where t is the time, $\pi = 3.1416$, l is the length of the pendulum, and g is the resultant acceleration1 produced by all the forces to which the pendulum is subject. If l is determined by measurement and t is found by observations, the resultant acceleration is given by

$$g = \frac{4\pi^2 l}{t^2}.$$

Consequently, the pendulum furnishes a means of finding the gravity g at any place.

In order to treat the problem of determining the shape of the earth from a knowledge of g at various places on its surface, suppose first that it is a homogeneous sphere. If this were its shape, its attraction would be equal for all points on its surface. But the gravity g would not be the same at all places, because it is the resultant of the earth's attraction and the centrifugal acceleration due to the earth's rotation. The gravity g would be the greatest at the poles, where there is no centrifugal acceleration, and least at the equator, where the attraction is exactly opposed by the centrifugal acceleration. Moreover, the value of g would vary from the poles to the equator in a perfectly definite manner which could easily be determined from theoretical considerations.

Now suppose the earth is oblate. It can be shown mathematically that the attraction of an oblate body for a particle at its pole is greater than that of a sphere of equal volume and density for a particle on its surface, and that at its equator the attraction is less. Therefore at the pole, where there is no centrifugal acceleration, g is greater on an oblate body than it is on an equal sphere. On the other hand, at the equator g is less on the oblate body than on the sphere both because the attraction of the former is less, and also because its equator is farther from its axis so that the centrifugal acceleration is greater.

That is, the manner in which g varies from pole to equator depends upon the oblateness of the earth, and it can be computed when the oblateness is given. Conversely, when g has been found by experiment, the shape of the earth can be computed. Very extensive determinations of g by means of the pendulum, taken in connection with the mathematical theory, not only prove that the earth is oblate, but give a degree of flattening agreeing closely with that obtained from the measurement of arcs. The question arises why g is determined by means of the pendulum. Its variations cannot be found by using balance scales, because the forces on both the body to be weighed and the counter weights vary in the same proportion.

However, the variations in g can be determined with some approximation by employing the spring balance. The choice between the spring balance and the pendulum is to be settled on the basis of convenience and accuracy. It is obvious that spring balances are very convenient, but they are not very accurate. On the other hand, the pendulum is capable of furnishing the variation of g with almost indefinite precision by the period in which it vibrates. Suppose the pendulum is moved from one place to another where g differs by one hundred-thousandth of its value. This small difference could not be detected by the use of spring balances, however many times the attempt might be made.

It follows from the formula that the time of a swing of the pendulum would be changed by about one two-hundredthousandth of its value. If the time of a complete oscillation were a second, for example, the difference could not be detected in a second; but the deviation for the following second would be equal to that in the first, and the difference would be doubled. The effect would accumulate, second after second, and in a day of 86, 400 seconds it would amount to nearly one half of a second, a quantity which is easily measured. In ten days the difference would amount to about 4.3 seconds.

The important point in the pendulum method is that the effects of the quantities to be measured accumulate until they become observable.

The Theoretical Shape of the Earth.—
The oblateness of the earth is not an accident; its shape depends on its size, mass, distribution of density, and rate of rotation. If it were homogeneous,

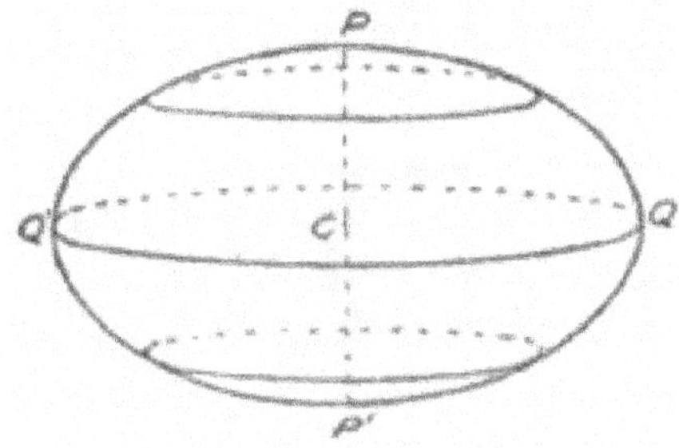

Fig.1 Oblate spheroid.

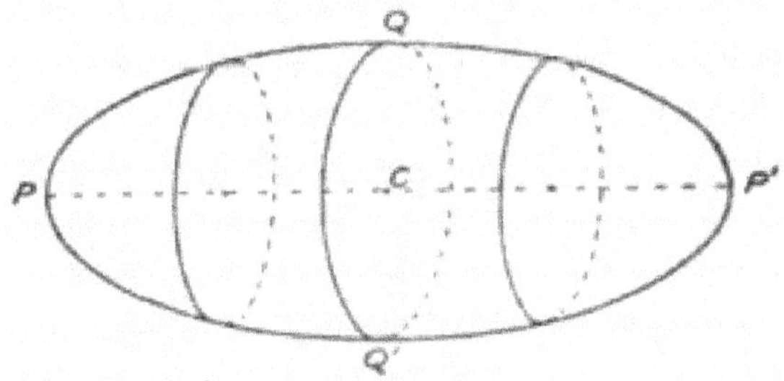

Fig. 2 Prolate spheroid.

its shape could be theoretically determined without great difficulty. It has been found from mathematical discussions that if a homogeneous fluid body is slowly rotating it may have either of two forms of equilibrium, one of which is nearly spherical while the other is very much flattened like a discus. These figures are not simply oblate, but they are figures known as spheroids. A spheroid is a solid generated by the rotation of an ellipse (Art. 53) about one of its diameters.

ers. Figure 1 is an oblate spheroid generated by the rotation of the ellipse P QP0Q0 about its shortest diameter P P0 . Its equator is its largest circumference. Figure 2 is a prolate spheroid generated by the rotation of the ellipse P QP0Q0 about its longest diameter P P0 . The equator of this figure is its smallest circumference. The oblate and prolate spheroids are fundamentally different in shape.

Of the two oblate spheroids which theory shows are figures of equilibrium for slow rotation, that which is the more nearly spherical is stable, while the other is unstable. That is, if the former were disturbed a little, it would retake its spheroidal form, while if the latter were deformed a little, it would take an entirely different shape, or might even break all to pieces. In spite of the fact that the earth is neither a fluid nor homogeneous, its shape is almost exactly that of the more nearly spherical oblate spheroid corresponding to its density and rate of rotation.

This fact might tempt one to the conclusion that it was formerly in a fluid state. But this conclusion is not necessarily sound, because, in such an enormous body, the strains which would result from appreciable departure from the figure of equilibrium would be so great that they could not be withstood by the strongest material known. Besides this, if the conditions for equilibrium were not exactly satisfied by the solid parts of the earth, the water and atmosphere would move and make compensation.

The sun, moon, and planets are bodies whose forms can likewise be compared with the results furnished by theory. Their figures agree closely with the theoretical forms. The only appreciable disagreements are in the case of Jupiter and Saturn, both of which are more nearly spherical than the corresponding homogeneous bodies would be. The reason for this is that these planets are very rare in their outer parts and relatively dense at their centers. It is probable that they are even more stable than the corresponding homogeneous figures.

Different Kinds of Latitude.—

It was seen in Art. 12 that perpendiculars to the water-level surface of the earth, except on the equator and at the poles, do not pass through the center of the earth. This leads to the definition of different kinds of latitude. The geometrically simplest latitude is that defined by a line from the center of the earth to the point on its surface occupied by the observer. Thus, in Fig. 3, P C is the earth's axis of rotation, QC is in the plane of its equator, and O is the position of the observer. The angle l is called the geocentric latitude.

The observer at O cannot see the center of the earth and cannot locate it by any kind of observation made at his station alone. Consequently, he cannot directly determine l. All he has is the perpendicular to the surface defined by his plumb line which strikes the line CQ at A. The angle l1 between this line and CQ is his astronomical latitude. The difference between the geocentric and astronomical latitudes varies from zero at the poles and equator to about 110 in latitude 45° .

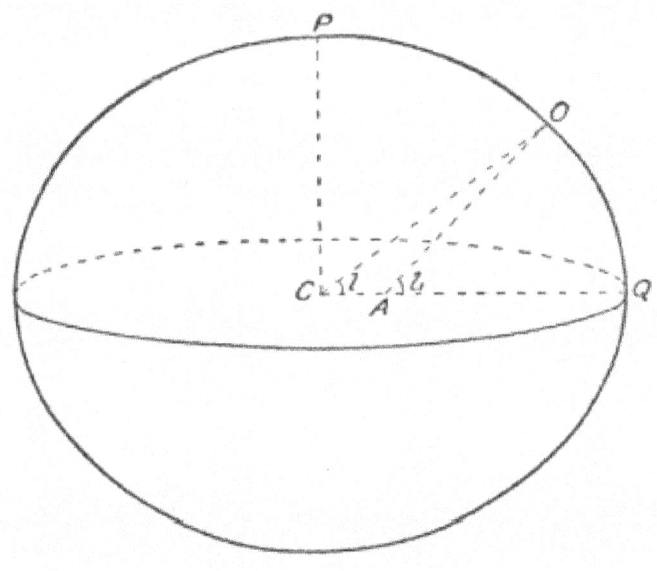

Fig.3 Geocentric and astronomical latitudes.

Sometimes the plumb line has an abnormal direction because of the attractions of neighboring mountains, or because of local excesses or deficiencies of matter under the surface. The astronomical latitude, when corrected for these anomalies, is called the geographical latitude. The astronomical and geographical latitudes rarely differ by more than a few seconds of arc.

II

THE MASS OF THE EARTH AND THE CONDITION OF ITS INTERIOR

The Principle by which Mass is Determined.—

It is important to understand clearly the principles which are at the foundation of any subject in which one may be interested, and this applies in the present problem. The ordinary method of determining the mass of a body is to weigh it. That is the way in which the quantity of most commodities, such as coal or ice or sugar, is found. The reason a body has weight at the surface of the earth is that the earth attracts it. It will be seen later (Art. 40) that the body attracts the earth equally in the opposite direction. Consequently, the real property of a body by which its mass is determined is its attraction for some other body.

The underlying principle is that the mass of a body is proportional to the attraction which it has for another body. Now consider the problem of finding the mass of the earth, which must be solved by considering its attraction for some other body. Its attraction for any given mass, for example, a cubic inch of iron, can easily be measured. But this does not give the mass of the earth compared to the cubic inch of iron. It is necessary to compare the attraction of the earth for the iron with the attraction of some other fully known body, as a lead ball of given size, for the same unit of iron.

Since the amount of attraction of one body for another depends upon their distance apart, it is necessary to measure the distance from the lead ball to the attracted body, and also to know the distance of the attracted body from the center of the earth. For this reason the mass of the earth could not be found until after its dimensions had been ascertained. By comparing the attractions of the earth and the lead ball for the attracted body, and making proper adjustments for the distances of their respective centers from it, the number of times the earth exceeds the lead ball in mass can be determined.

Not only is the mass of the earth computed from its attraction, but the same principle is the basis for determining the mass of every other celestial body. The masses of those planets that have satellites are easily found from their attractions for their respective satellites, and when two stars revolve around each other in known orbits their masses are defined by their mutual attractions. There is no means of determining the mass of a single star.

The Mass and Density of the Earth.—

By applications (Arts. 21, 22) of the principle in Art. 19 the mass of the earth has been found. If it were weighed a small quantity at a time at the surface, its total weight in tons would be 6×10^{21}, or 6 followed by 21 ciphers. This makes no appeal to the imagination because the numbers are so extremely far beyond all experience. A much better method is to give its density, which is obtained by dividing its mass by its volume. With water at its greatest density as a standard, the average density of the earth is 5.53. The average density of the earth to the depth of a mile or two is in the neighborhood of 2.75.

Therefore there are much denser materials in the earth's interior; their greater density may be due either to their composition or to the great pressure to which they are subject. The density of quartz (sand) is 2.75, limestone 3.2, cast iron 7.1, steel 7.8, lead 11.3, mercury 13.6, gold 19.3, and platinum 21.5. It follows that no considerable part of the earth can be composed of such heavy substances as mercury, gold, and platinum, but, so far as these considerations bear on the question, it might be largely iron.

The distribution of density in the earth was worked out over 100 years ago by Laplace on the basis of a certain assumption regarding the compressibility of the matter of which it is composed. The results of this computation have been compared with all the phenomena on which the disposition of the mass of the earth has an influence, and the results have been very satisfactory. Hence, it is supposed that this law represents approximately the way the density of the earth increases from its surface to its center. According to this law, taking the density of the surface as 2.72, the densities at depths of 1000, 2000, 3000 miles, and the center of the earth are respectively 5.62, 8.30, 10.19, 10.87. At no depth is the average density so great as that of the heavier metals.

Determination of the Density of the Earth by Means of the Torsion Balance.—

The whole difficulty in determining the density of the earth is due to the fact that the attractions of masses of moderate dimensions are so feeble that they almost escape detection with the most sensitive apparatus. The problem from an experimental point of view reduces to that of devising a means of measuring extremely minute forces. It has been solved most successfully by the torsion balance. The torsion balance consists essentially of two small balls, bb in Fig. 14, connected by a rod which is suspended from the point O by a quartz fiber OA.

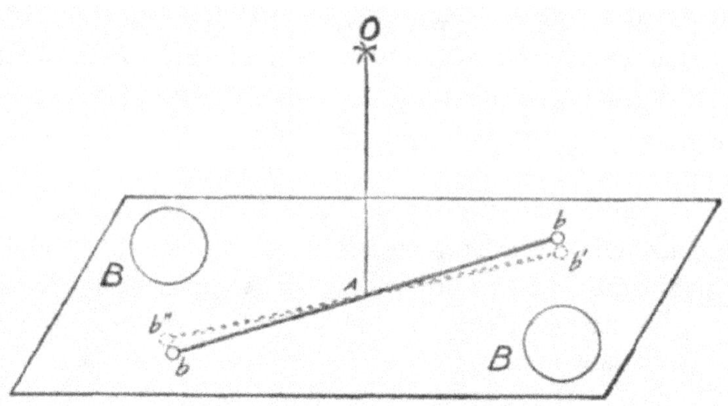

The torsion balance.

If the apparatus is left for a considerable time in a sealed case so that it is not disturbed by air currents, it comes to rest. Suppose the balls bb are at rest and that the large balls BB are carefully brought near them on opposite sides of the connecting rod, as shown in the figure. They exert slight attractions for the small balls and gradually move them against the feeble resistance of the quartz fiber to torsion (twisting) to the position b 0 b 00. The resistance of the quartz fiber becomes greater the more it is twisted, and finally exactly balances the attraction of the large balls.

The forces involved are so small that several hours may be required for the balls to reach their final positions of rest. But they will finally be reached and the angle through which the rod has been turned can be recorded. The next problem is to determine from the deflection which the large balls have produced how great the force is which they have exerted. This would be a simple matter if it were known how much resistance the quartz fiber offers to twisting, but the resistance is so exceedingly small that it cannot be directly determined.

However, it can be found by a very interesting indirect method. Suppose the large balls are removed and that the rod connecting the small balls is twisted a little out of its position of equilibrium. It will then turn back because of the resistance offered to twisting by the quartz fiber, and will rotate past the position of equilibrium almost as far as it was originally displaced in the opposite direction. Then it will return and vibrate back and forth until friction destroys its motion. It is evident that the characteristics of the oscillations are much like those of a vibrating pendulum. The formula connecting the various quantities involved is

$$t = 2\pi \sqrt{l/f},$$

where t is the time of a complete oscillation of the rod joining b and b, l is the distance from A to b, and f is the resistance of torsion. This equation differs from that for the pendulum, Art. 15, only in that g has been replaced by f. Now l is measured, t is observed, and f is computed from the equation with great exactness however small it may be. Now that f and g are known it is easy to compute the mass of the earth by means of the law of gravitation (Art. 146). Let E represent the mass of the earth, R its radius, 2B the mass of the two large balls, and r the distances from BB to bb respectively. Then, since gravitation is proportional to the attracting mass and inversely as the square of its distance from the attracted body,

$$\frac{E}{R^2} : \frac{2B}{r^2} = g : f.$$

In this proportion the only unknown is E, which can therefore be computed.

Determination of the Density of the Earth by the Mountain Method.—

The characteristic of the torsion balance is that it is very delicate and adapted to measuring very small forces; the characteristic of the mountain method is that a very large mass is employed, and the forces are larger. In the torsion balance the balls BB are brought near those suspended by the quartz fiber and are removed at will. A mountain cannot be moved, and the advantage of using a large mass is at least partly counterbalanced by this disadvantage. The necessity for moving the attracting body (in this case the mountain) is obviated in a very ingenious manner.

For simplicity let the oblateness of the earth be neglected in explaining the mountain method. In Fig. 15, C is the center of the earth, M is the mountain, and O1 and O2 are two stations on opposite sides of the mountain at which plumb lines are suspended. If it were not for the attraction of the mountain they would hang in the directions O1C and O2C. The angle between these lines at C depends upon the distance between the stations O1 and O2. The distance between these stations, even though they are on opposite sides of the mountain, can be obtained by triangulation. Then, since the size of the earth is known, the angle at C can be computed.

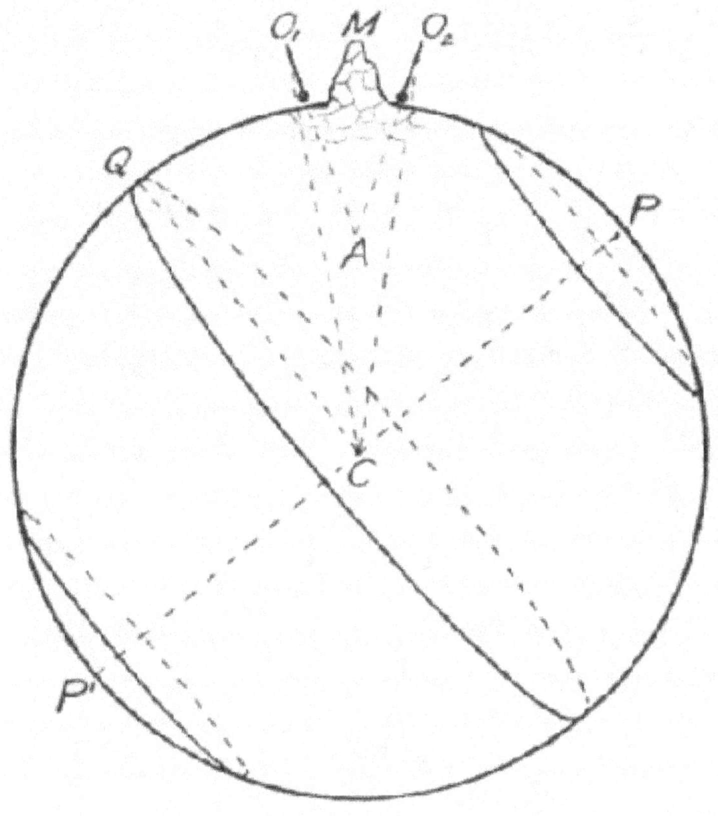

The mountain method of determining the mass of the earth.

But the attraction of the mountain for the plumb bobs causes the plumb lines to hang in the directions O1A and O2A. The directions of these lines with respect to the stars can easily be determined by observations, and the difference in their directions as thus determined is the angle at A. What is desired is the deflections of the plumb line produced by the attractions of the mountain. It follows from elementary geometry that the sum of the two small deflections CO1A and CO2A equals the angle A minus the angle C.

Suppose, for simplicity, that the mountain is symmetrical and that the deflections are equal. Then each one equals one half the difference of the angles A and C. Therefore the desired quantities have been found. When the deflection has been found it is easy to obtain the relation of the force exerted by the mountain to that due to the earth. Let Fig. represent the plumb line on a large scale. If it were not for the mountain it would hang in the direction O_1B_1; it actually hangs in the direction $O_1B_0{}_1$. The earth's attraction is in the direction O_1B_1, and that of the mountain is in the direction $B_1B_0{}_1$. The two forces are in the same ratio as O_1B_1 is to $B_1B_0{}_1$, for, by the law of the composition of forces, only then would the plumb line hang in the direction $O_1B_0{}_1$.

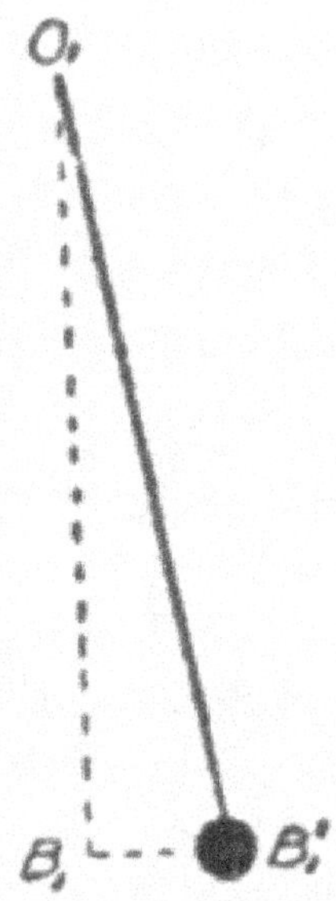

The deflection of a plumb line.

The problem of finding the mass of the earth compared to that of the mountain now proceeds just like that of finding the mass of the earth compared to the balls BB in the torsion-balance method. The mountain plays the rôle of the large balls. A mountain 5000 feet high and broad would cause nearly 800 times as much deflection as that produced by an iron ball a foot in diameter. The advantage of the large deflection is offset by not having very accurate means of measuring it, and also by the fact that it is necessary to determine the mass of a more or less irregular shaped mountain made up of materials which may lack much of being uniform in density. In spite of these drawbacks this method was the first one to give fairly accurate results.

Determination of the Density of the Earth by the Pendulum Method.—

It was explained in Art. 15 that the pendulum furnishes a very accurate means of determining the force of gravity. Its delicacy arises from the fact that in using it the effects of the changes in the forces accumulate indefinitely; no such favorable circumstances were present in the methods of the torsion balance and the mountain. Suppose a pendulum has been swung at the surface of the earth so long that the period of its oscillation has been accurately determined. Then suppose it is taken at the same place down into a deep pit or mine. The force to which it is subject will be changed for three different reasons.

(a) The pendulum will be nearer the axis of rotation of the earth and the centrifugal acceleration to which it is subject will be diminished. The relative change in gravity due to this cause can be accurately computed from the latitude of the position and the depth of the pit or mine. (b) The pendulum will be nearer the center of the earth, and, so far as this factor alone is concerned, the force to which it is subject will be increased. Moreover, the relative change due to this cause also can be computed. (c) The pendulum will be below a certain amount of material whose attraction will now be in the opposite direction.

This cannot be computed directly because the amount of attraction due to a ton of matter, for example, is unknown. This is what is to be found out. But from the time of the oscillation of the pendulum at the bottom of the pit or mine the whole force to which it is subject can be computed. Then, on making correction for the known changes (a) and (b), the unknown change (c) can be obtained simply by subtraction. From the amount of force exerted by the known mass above the pendulum, the density of the earth can be computed by essentially the same process as that employed in the case of the torsion-balance method and the mountain method.

Temperature and Pressure in the Earth's Interior.—

There are many reasons for believing that the interior of the earth is very hot. For example, volcanic phenomena prove that at least in many localities the temperature is above the melting point of rock at a comparatively short distance below the earth's surface. Geysers and hot springs show that the interior of the earth is hot at many other places. Besides this, the temperature has been found to rise in deep mines at the rate of about one degree Fahrenheit for a descent of 100 feet, the amount depending somewhat on the locality. Suppose the temperature should go on increasing at the rate of one degree for every hundred feet from the surface to the center of the earth.

At a depth of ten miles it would be over 500 degrees, at 100 miles over 5000 degrees, at 1000 miles over 50, 000 degrees, and at the center of the earth over 200, 000 degrees. While there is no probability that the rate of increase of temperature which prevails near the surface keeps up to great depths, yet it is reasonably certain that at a depth of a few hundred miles it is several thousand degrees. Since almost every substance melts at a temperature below 5000 degrees, it has been supposed until recent times that the interior of the earth, below the depth of 100 miles, is liquid.

But the great pressure to which matter in the interior of the earth is subject is a factor that cannot safely be neglected. A cylinder one inch in cross section and 1728 inches, or 144 feet, in height has a volume of one cubic foot. If it is filled with water, the pressure on the bottom equals the weight of a cubic foot of water, or 62.5 pounds. The pressure per square inch on the bottom of the column 144 feet high having the density 2.75, or that of the earth's crust, is

172 pounds. The pressure per square inch at the depth of a mile is 6300 pounds, or 3 tons in round numbers.

The pressure is approximately proportional to the depth for a considerable distance. Therefore, the pressure per square inch at the depth of 100 miles is approximately 300 tons, and at 1000 miles it is 3000 tons. However, the pressure is not strictly proportional to the depth, and more refined means must be employed to find how great it is at the earth's center. Moreover, the pressure at great depths depends upon the distribution of mass in the earth. On the basis of the Laplacian law of density, which probably is a good approximation to the truth, the pressure per square inch at the center of the earth is 3, 000, 000 times the atmospheric pressure at the earth's surface, or 22, 500 tons.

It is a familiar fact that pressure increases the boiling points of liquids. It has been found recently by experiment that pressure increases the melting points of solids. Therefore, in view of the enormous pressures at moderate depths in the earth, it is not safe to conclude that its interior is molten without further evidence. The question cannot be answered directly because, in the first place, there is no very exact means of determining the temperature, and, in the second place, it is not possible to make experiments at such high pressures. There are, however, several methods of proving that the earth is solid through and through, and they will now be considered.

Proof of the Rigidity and Elasticity of the Earth by the Tide Experiment.—

Among the several lines of attack that have been made on the question of the rigidity of the earth, the one depending on the tides generated in the earth by the moon and sun has been most satisfactory; and of the methods of this class, that devised by Michelson and carried out in collaboration with Gale, in 1913, has given by far the most exact results. Besides, it has settled one very important question, which no other method has been able to answer, namely, that the earth is highly elastic instead of being viscous. For these reasons the work of Michelson and Gale will be treated first.

The important difference between a solid and a liquid is that the former offers resistance to deforming forces while the latter does not. If a perfect solid existed, no force whatever could deform it; if a perfect liquid existed, the only resistance it would offer to deformation would be the inertia of the parts moved. Neither perfect solids nor absolutely perfect liquids are known. If a solid body has the property of being deformed more and more by a continually applied force, and if, on the application of the force being discontinued, the body not only does not retake its original form but does not even tend toward it, then it is said to be viscous.

Putty is a good example of a material that is viscous. On the other hand, if on the application of a continuous force the body is deformed to a certain extent beyond which it does not go, and if, on the removal of the force, it returns absolutely to its original condition, it is said to be elastic. While there are no solid bodies which are either perfectly viscous or perfectly elastic, the distinction is a clear and important one, and the characteristics of a solid may be described by stating how far it approaches one or the other of these ideal states. In order to find how the earth is deformed by forces it is necessary to consider what forces there are acting on it.

The most obvious ones are the attractions of the sun and moon. But it is not clear in the first place that these attractions tend to deform the earth, and in the second place that, even if they have such a tendency, the result is at all appreciable. A ball of iron attracted by a magnet is not sensibly deformed, and it seems that the earth should behave similarly. But the earth is so large that one's intuitions utterly fail in such considerations. The sun and moon actually do tend to alter the shape of the earth, and the amount of its deformation due to their attractions is measurable. The forces are precisely those that produce the tides in the ocean.

It will be sufficient at present to give a rough idea, correct so far as it goes, of the reason that the moon and sun raise tides in the earth, reserving for Arts. 263, 264 a more complete treatment of the question. In Fig. 17 let E represent the center of the earth, the arrow the direction toward the moon, and A and B the points where the line from E to the moon pierces the earth's surface. The moon is 4000 miles nearer to A than it is to E, and 4000 miles nearer to E than it is to B.

Therefore the attraction of the moon for a unit mass at A is greater than it is for a unit mass at E, and greater for a unit mass at E than it is for one at B. Since the distance from the earth to the moon is 240, 000 miles, the distance of the moon from A is fifty-nine sixtieths of its distance from E. Since the attraction varies inversely as the square of the distance, the force on A is about one thirtieth greater than that on E, and the difference between the forces on E and B is only slightly less.

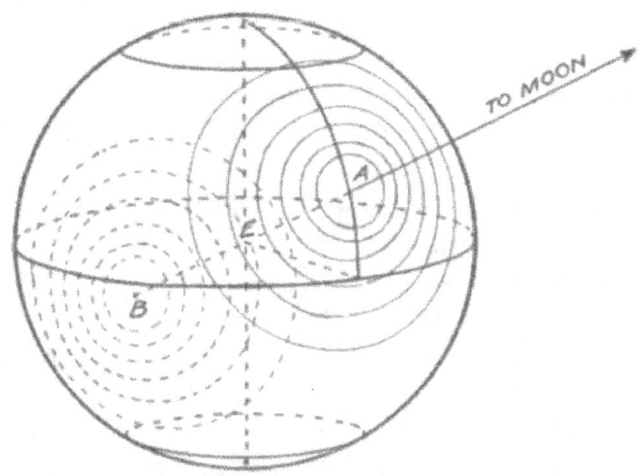

The tidal bulges at A and B on the earth produced by the moon.

It follows from the relation of the attraction of the moon for masses at A, E, and B that it tends to pull the nearer material at A away from the center of the earth E, and the center of the earth away from the more remote material at B. Since the forces are known, it is possible to compute the elongation the earth would suffer if it were a perfect fluid. The result is two elevations, or tidal bulges, at A and B. The concentric lines shown in Fig. 17 are the lines of equal elevation. A rather difficult mathematical discussion shows that the radii EA and EB would each be lengthened by about four feet. Since the earth possesses at least some degree of rigidity its actual tidal elongation is somewhat less than four feet. When it is remembered that the uncertainty in the diameter of the earth, in spite of the many years that have been devoted to determining it, is still several hundred feet, the problem of finding how much the earth's elongation, as a consequence of the rapidly changing tidal forces, falls short of four feet seems altogether hopeless of solution. Nevertheless the problem has been solved.

Suppose a pipe half filled with water is fastened in a horizontal position to the surface of the earth. The water in the pipe is subject to the attraction of the moon. To fix the ideas, suppose the pipe lies in the east-and-west direction in the same latitude as the point A, Fig. . Suppose, first, that the earth is absolutely rigid so that it is not deformed by the moon, and consider what happens to the water in the pipe as the rotation of the earth carries it past the point A. When the pipe is to the west of A the water rises in its eastern end, and settles correspondingly in its western end, because the moon tends to make an elevation on the earth at A. When the pipe is carried past A to the east the water rises in its western end and settles in its eastern end. Since the earth is not absolutely rigid the magnitudes of the tides under the hypothesis that it is rigid cannot be experimentally determined; but, since all the forces that are involved are known, the heights the tides would be on a rigid earth can be computed.

Suppose now that the earth yields perfectly to the disturbing forces of the moon. Its surface is in this case always the exact figure of equilibrium. Consider the pipe, which is attached to this surface, when it is to the west of A. The water would be high in its eastern end if the shape of the surface of the earth were unchanged. But the surface to the east of it is elevated and the pipe is raised with it. Moreover, the elevation of the surface is, under the present hypothesis, just that necessary for equilibrium. Therefore, in this case there is no tide at all with respect to the pipe.

The actual earth is neither absolutely rigid nor perfectly fluid. Consequently the tides in the pipe will actually be neither their theoretical maximum nor zero. The amount by which they fall short of the value they would have if the earth were perfectly rigid depends upon the extent to which it yields to the moon's forces, and is a measure of this yielding. Therefore the problem of finding how much the earth is deformed by the moon is reduced to computing how great the tides in the pipe would be if the earth were absolutely rigid, and then comparing these results with the actual tides in the pipe as determined by direct experiment. After the amount the earth yields has been determined in this way, its rigidity can be found by the theory of the deformation of solid bodies.

In the experiment of Michelson and Gale two pipes were used, one lying in the plane of the meridian and the other in the east-and-west direction. In order to secure freedom from vibrations due to trains and heavy wagons they were placed on the grounds of the Yerkes Observatory, and to avoid variations in temperature they were buried a number of feet in the ground. Since the tidal forces are very small, pipes 500 feet long were used, and even then the maximum tides were only about two thousandths of an inch. An ingenious method of measuring these small changes in level was devised. The ends of the pipes were sealed with plane glass windows.

through which their interiors could be viewed. Sharp pointers, fastened to the pipe, were placed just under the surface of the water near the windows. When viewed from below the level of the water the pointer and its reflected image could be seen. Figure 18 shows an end of one of the pipes, S is the surface of the water, P is the pointer, and P 0 is its reflected image. The distances of P and P 0 from the surface S are equal. Now suppose the water rises; since P and P 0 are equidistant from S, the change in their apparent distance is twice the change in the water level. The distances between P and P 0 were accurately measured with the help of permanently fixed microscopes, and the variations in the water level were determined within one per cent of their whole amount.

In order to make clear the accuracy of the results, the complicated nature of the tides must be pointed out. Consider the tidal bulges A and B, Fig. 17, which give an idea of what happened to the water in the pipes. For simplicity, fix the attention on the eastand-west pipe, which in the experiment was about 13° north of the highest latitude A ever attains. The rotating earth carried it daily across the meridian of A to the north of A, and similarly across the meridian of B. When the relations were as represented in the diagram there were considerable tides in the pipe before and after it crossed the meridian at A because it was, so to speak, well on the tidal bulge. On the other hand, when it crossed the meridian of B about 12 hours later, the tides were very small because the bulge B was far south of the equator.

But the moon was not all the time north of the plane of the earth's equator. Once each month it was 28° north and once each month 28° south, and it varied from hour to hour in a rather irregular manner. Moreover, its distance, on which the magnitudes of the tidal forces depend, also changed continuously. Then add to all these complexities the corresponding ones due to the sun, which are unrelated to those of the moon, and which mix up with them and make the phenomena still more involved.

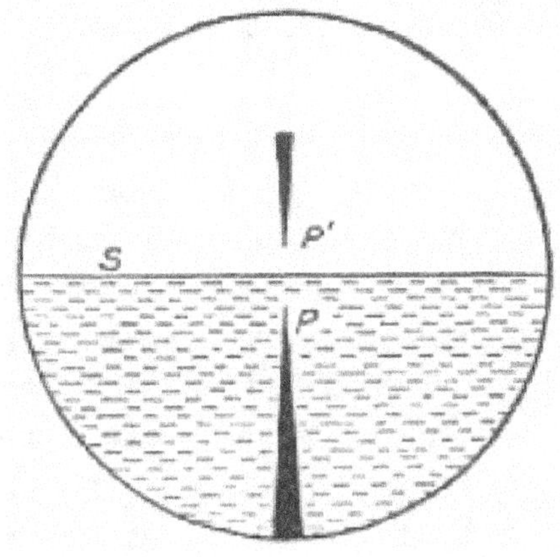

End of pipe in the Michelson-Gale tide experiment.

Finally, consider the north-and-south pipe and notice, by the help of Fig. , that its tides are altogether distinct in character from those in the east-and-west pipe. With all this in mind, remember that the observations made every two hours of the day for a period of several months agreed perfectly in all their characteristics with the results given by theory. The only difference was that the observed tides were reduced in a constant ratio by the yielding of the earth.

The perfection of this domain of science is proved by the satisfactory coördination in this experiment of a great many distinct theories. The perfect agreement in their characteristics of more than a thousand observed tides with their computed values depended on the correctness of the laws of motion, the truth of the law of gravitation, the size of the earth, the distance of the moon and the theory of its motion, the mass of the moon, the distance to the sun and the theory of the earth's motion around it, the mass of the sun, the theory of tides, the numerous observations, and the lengthy calculations. How improbable that there would be perfect harmony between observation and theory in so many cases unless scientific conclusions respecting all these things are correct!

The extent to which the earth yields to the forces of the moon was obtained from the amount by which the observed tides were less than their theoretical values for an unyielding earth. It was found that in the east-and-west pipe the observed tides were about 70 per cent of the computed, while in the north-and-south pipe the observed tides were only about 50 per cent of the computed. This led to the astonishing conclusion, which, however, had been reached earlier by Schweydar on the basis of much less certain observational data, that the earth's resistance to deformation in the east-and-west direction is greater than it is in the north-and-south direction. Love has suggested that the difference may be due indirectly to the effects of the oceanic tides on the general body of the earth.

III

CELESTIAL POLES AND CELESTIAL EQUATOR

To help orient us in the turning sky, astronomers use a system that extends Earth's axis points into the sky. Imagine a line going through Earth, connecting the North and South Poles. This is Earth's axis, and Earth rotates about this line. If we extend this imaginary line outward from Earth, the points where this line intersects the celestial sphere are called the north celestial pole and the south celestial pole. As Earth rotates about its axis, the sky appears to turn in the opposite direction around those celestial poles (Figure). We also (in our imagination) throw Earth's equator onto the sky and call this the celestial equator. It lies halfway between the celestial poles, just as Earth's equator lies halfway between our planet's poles.

Circling the South Celestial Pole. This long-exposure photo shows trails left by stars as a result of the apparent rotation of the celestial sphere around the south celestial pole. (In reality, it is Earth that rotates.)

Now let's imagine how riding on different parts of our spinning Earth affects our view of the sky. The apparent motion of the celestial sphere depends on your latitude (position north or south of the equator). First of all, notice that Earth's axis is pointing at the celestial poles, so these two points in the sky do not appear to turn. If you stood at the North Pole of Earth, for example, you would see the north celestial pole overhead, at your zenith. The celestial equator, 90° from the celestial poles, would lie along your horizon. As you watched the stars during the course of the night, they would all circle around the celestial pole, with none rising or setting. Only that half of the sky north of the celestial equator is ever visible to an observer at the North Pole. Similarly, an observer at the South Pole would see only the southern half of the sky.

If you were at Earth's equator, on the other hand, you see the celestial equator (which, after all, is just an "extension" of Earth's equator) pass overhead through your zenith. The celestial poles, being 90° from the celestial equator, must then be at the north and south points on your horizon. As the sky turns, all stars riseand set; they move straight up from the east side of the horizon and set straight down on the west side. During a 24-hour period, all stars are above the horizon exactly half the time. (Of course, during some of those hours, the Sun is too bright for us to see them.)

What would an observer in the latitudes of the United States or Europe see? Remember, we are neither at Earth's pole nor at the equator, but in between them. For those in the continental United States and Europe, the north celestial pole is neither overhead nor on the horizon, but in between. It appears above the northern horizon at an angular height, or altitude, equal to the observer's latitude. In San Francisco, for example, where the latitude is 38° N, the north celestial pole is 38° above the northern horizon. For an observer at 38° N latitude, the south celestial pole is 38° below the southern horizon and, thus, never visible. As Earth turns, the whole sky seems to pivot about the north celestial pole.

For this observer, stars within 38° of the North Pole can never set. They are always above the horizon, day and night. This part of the sky is called the north circumpolar zone. For observers in the continental United States, the Big Dipper, Little Dipper, and Cassiopeia are examples of star groups in the north circumpolar zone. On the other hand, stars within 38° of the south celestial pole never rise. That part of the sky is the south circumpolar zone. To most U.S. observers, the Southern Cross is in that zone. (Don't worry if you are not familiar with the star groups just mentioned; we will introduce them more formally later on.)

At this particular time in Earth's history, there happens to be a star very close to the north celestial pole. It is called Polaris, the pole star, and has the distinction of being the star that moves the least amount as the northern sky turns each day. Because it moved so little while the other stars moved much more, it played a special role in the mythology of several Native American tribes, for example (some called it the "fastener of the sky").

IV
RISING AND SETTING OF THE SUN

We described the movement of stars in the night sky, but what about during the daytime? The stars continue to circle during the day, but the brilliance of the Sun makes them difficult to see. (The Moon can often be seen in the daylight, however.) On any given day, we can think of the Sun as being located at some position on the hypothetical celestial sphere. When the Sun rises—that is, when the rotation of Earth carries the Sun above the horizon—sunlight is scattered by the molecules of our atmosphere, filling our sky with light and hiding the stars above the horizon.

For thousands of years, astronomers have been aware that the Sun does more than just rise and set. It changes position gradually on the celestial sphere, moving each day about 1° to the east relative to the stars. Very reasonably, the ancients thought this meant the Sun was slowly moving around Earth, taking a period of time we call 1 year to make a full circle. Today, of course, we know it is Earth that is going around the Sun, but the effect is the same: the Sun's position in our sky changes day to day. We have a similar experience when we walk around a campfire at night; we see the flames appear in front of each person seated about the fire in turn.

The path the Sun appears to take around the celestial sphere each year is called the ecliptic (Figure). Because of its motion on the ecliptic, the Sun rises about 4 minutes later each day with respect to the stars. Earth must make just a bit more than one complete rotation (with respect to the stars) to bring the Sun up again.

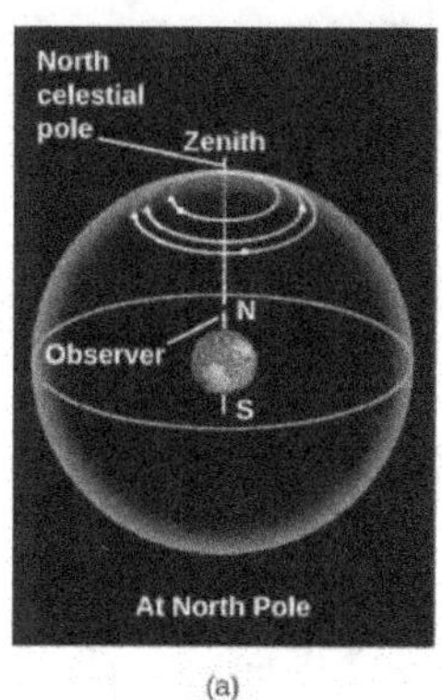

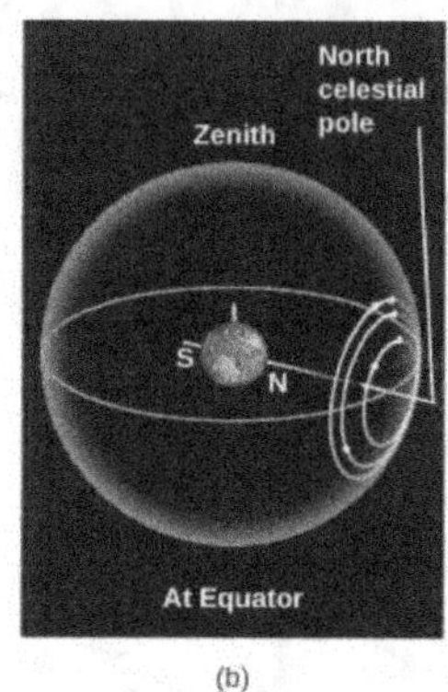

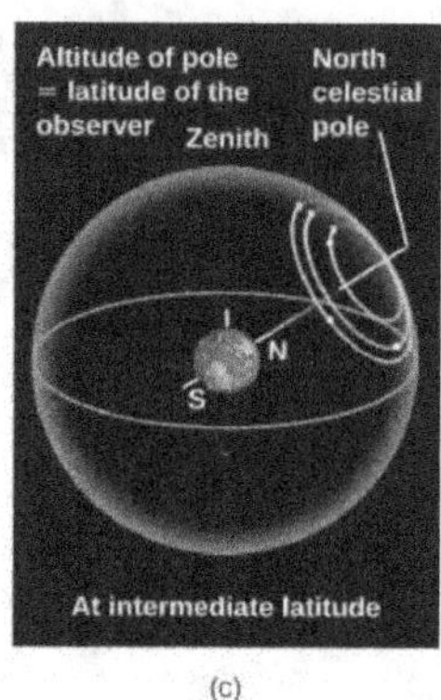

Star Circles at Different Latitudes. The turning of the sky looks different depending on your latitude on Earth. (a) At the North Pole, the stars circle the zenith and do not rise and set. (b) At the equator, the celestial poles are on the horizon, and the stars rise straight up and set straight down. (c) At intermediate latitudes, the north celestial pole is at some position between overhead and the horizon. Its angle above the horizon turns out to be equal to the observer's latitude. Stars rise and set at an angle to the horizon.

As the months go by and we look at the Sun from different places in our orbit, we see it projected against different places in our orbit, and thus against different stars in the background (Figure and Table)—or we would, at least, if we could see the stars in the daytime. In practice, we must deduce which stars lie behind and beyond the Sun by observing the stars visible in the opposite direction at night. After a year, when Earth has completed one trip around the Sun, the

Sun will appear to have completed one circuit of the sky along the ecliptic.

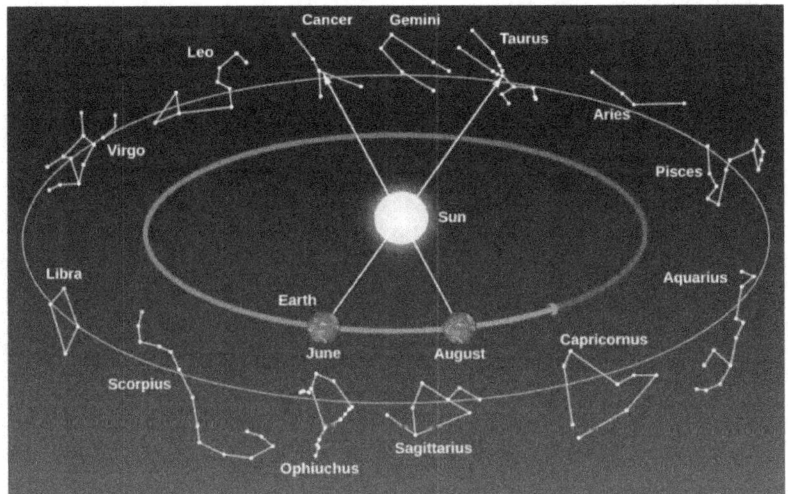

Constellations on the Ecliptic. As Earth revolves around the Sun, we sit on "platform Earth" and see the Sun moving around the sky. The circle in the sky that the Sun appears to make around us in the course of a year is called the ecliptic. This circle (like all circles in the sky) goes through a set of constellations. The ancients thought these constellations, which the Sun (and the Moon and planets) visited, must be special and incorporated them into their system of astrology. Note that at any given time of the year, some of the constellations crossed by the ecliptic are visible in the night sky; others are in the day sky and are thus hidden by the brilliance of the Sun.

Constellation on the Ecliptic	Dates When the Sun Crosses It
Capricornus	January 21–February 16
Aquarius	February 16–March 11
Pisces	March 11–April 18
Aries	April 18–May 13
Taurus	May 13–June 22
Gemini	June 22–July 21
Cancer	July 21–August 10
Leo	August 10–September 16
Virgo	September 16–October 31

Constellation on the Ecliptic	Dates When the Sun Crosses It
Libra	October 31–November 23
Scorpius	November 23–November 29
Ophiuchus	November 29–December 18
Sagittarius	December 18–January 21

The ecliptic does not lie along the celestial equator but is inclined to it at an angle of about 23.5°. In other words, the Sun's annual path in the sky is not linked with Earth's equator. This is because our planet's axis of rotation is tilted by about 23.5° from a vertical line sticking out of the plane of the ecliptic (Figure). Being tilted from "straight up" is not at all unusual among celestial bodies; Uranus and Pluto are actually tilted so much that they orbit the Sun "on their side."

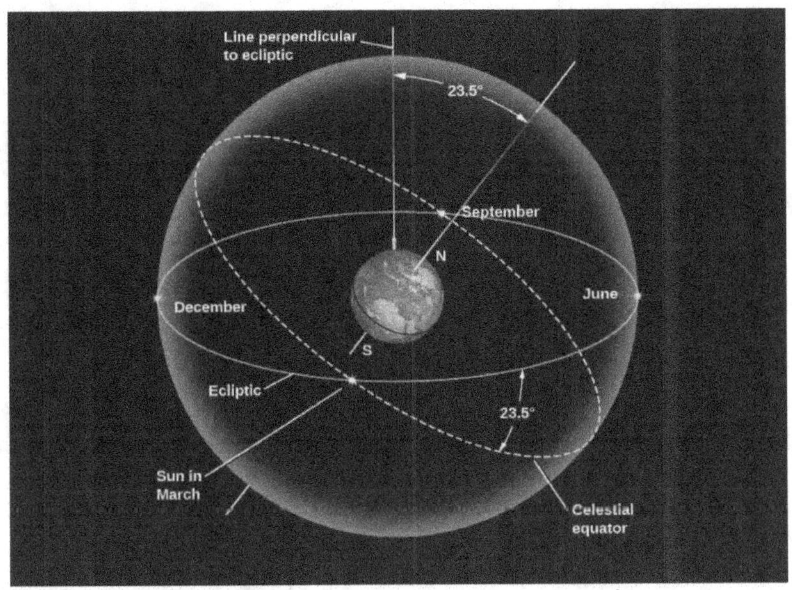

The Celestial Tilt. The celestial equator is tilted by 23.5° to the ecliptic. As a result, North Americans and Europeans see the Sun north of the celestial equator and high in our sky in June, and south of the celestial equator and low in the sky in December.

The inclination of the ecliptic is the reason the Sun moves north and south in the sky as the seasons change. In Earth, Moon, and Sky, we discuss the progression of the seasons in more detail.

Fixed and Wandering Stars

The Sun is not the only object that moves among the fixed stars. The Moon and each of the planets that are visible to the unaided eye—Mercury, Venus, Mars, Jupiter, Saturn, and Uranus (although just barely)—also change their positions slowly from day to day. During a single day, the Moon and planets all rise and set as Earth turns, just as the Sun and stars do. But like the Sun, they have independent motions among the stars, superimposed on the daily rotation of the celestial sphere. Noticing these motions, the Greeks of 2000 years ago distinguished between what they called the fixed stars—those that maintain fixed patterns among themselves through many generations—and the wandering stars, or planets.

The word "planet," in fact, means "wanderer" in ancient Greek. Today, we do not regard the Sun and Moon as planets, but the ancients applied the term to all seven of the moving objects in the sky. Much of ancient astronomy was devoted to observing and predicting the motions of these celestial wanderers. They even dedicated a unit of time, the week, to the seven objects that move on their own; that's why there are 7 days in a week. The Moon, being Earth's nearest celestial neighbor, has the fastest apparent motion; it completes a trip around the sky in about 1 month (or moonth). To do this, the Moon moves about 12°, or 24 times its own apparent width on the sky, each day.

The individual paths of the Moon and planets in the sky all lie close to the ecliptic, although not exactly on it. This is because the paths of the planets about the Sun, and of the Moon about Earth, are all in nearly the same plane, as if they were circles on a huge sheet of paper. The planets, the Sun, and the Moon are thus always found in the sky within a narrow 18-degree-wide belt, centered on the ecliptic, called the zodiac (Figure).

(The root of the term "zodiac" is the same as that of the word "zoo" and means a collection of animals; many of the patterns of stars within the zodiac belt reminded the ancients of animals, such as a fish or a goat.) How the planets appear to move in the sky as the months pass is a combination of their actual motions plus the motion of Earth about the Sun; consequently, their paths are somewhat complex. As we will see, this complexity has fascinated and challenged astronomers for centuries.

Constellations

The backdrop for the motions of the "wanderers" in the sky is the canopy of stars. If there were no clouds in the sky and we were on a flat plain with nothing to obstruct our view, we could see about 3000 stars with the unaided eye. To find their way around such a multitude, the ancients found groupings of stars that made some familiar geometric pattern or (more rarely) resembled something they knew. Each civilization found its own patterns in the stars, much like a modern Rorschach test in which you are asked to discern patterns or pictures in a set of inkblots. The ancient Chinese, Egyptians, and Greeks, among others, found their own groupings—or constellations—of stars.

These were helpful in navigating among the stars and in passing their star lore on to their children. You may be familiar with some of the old star patterns we still use today, such as the Big Dipper, Little Dipper, and Orion the hunter, with his distinctive belt of three stars (Figure). However, many of the stars we see are not part of a distinctive star pattern at all, and a telescope reveals millions of stars too faint for the eye to see. Therefore, during the early decades of the 20th century, astronomers from many countries decided to establish a more formal system for organizing the sky.

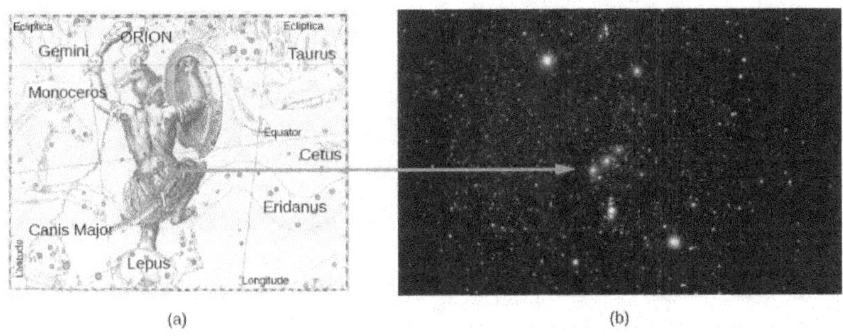

(a)   (b)

Orion. (a) The winter constellation of Orion, the hunter, is surrounded by neighboring constellations, as illustrated in the seventeenth-century atlas by Hevelius. (b) A photograph shows the Orion region in the sky. Note the three blue stars that make up the belt of the hunter. The bright red star above the belt denotes his armpit and is called Betelgeuse (pronounced "Beetel-juice"). The bright blue star below the belt is his foot and is called Rigel. (credit a: modification of work by Johannes Hevelius; b: modification of work by Matthew Spinelli)

V
THE LAWS OF PLANETARY MOTION

The First Two Laws of Planetary Motion

The path of an object through space is called its orbit. Kepler initially assumed that the orbits of planets were circles, but doing so did not allow him to find orbits that were consistent with Brahe's observations. Working with the data for Mars, he eventually discovered that the orbit of that planet had the shape of a somewhat flattened circle, or ellipse. Next to the circle, the ellipse is the simplest kind of closed curve, belonging to a family of curves known as conic sections

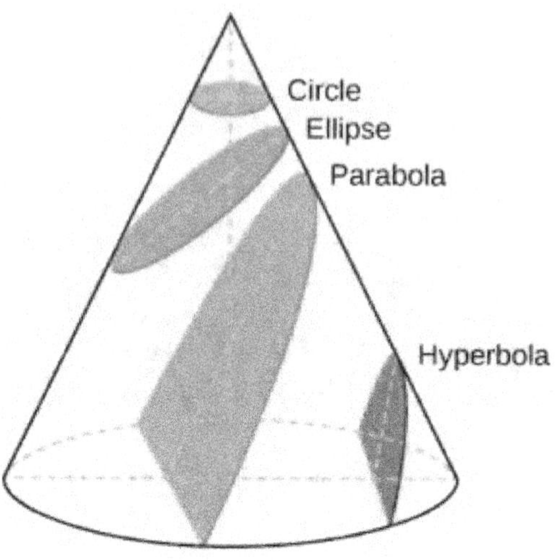

Conic Sections. The circle, ellipse, parabola, and hyperbola are all formed by the intersection of a plane with a cone. This is why such curves are called conic sections.

You might recall from math classes that in a circle, the center is a special point. The distance from the center to anywhere on the circle is exactly the same. In an ellipse, the sum of the distance from two special points inside the ellipse to any point on the ellipse is always the same. These two points inside the ellipse are called its foci (singular: focus), a word invented for this purpose by Kepler. This property suggests a simple way to draw an ellipse (Figure).

We wrap the ends of a loop of string around two tacks pushed through a sheet of paper into a drawing board, so that the string is slack. If we push a pencil against the string, making the string taut, and then slide the pencil against the string all around the tacks, the curve that results is an ellipse. At any point where the pencil may be, the sum of the distances from the pencil to the two tacks is a constant length—the length of the string. The tacks are at the two foci of the ellipse. The widest diameter of the ellipse is called its major axis.

Half this distance—that is, the distance from the center of the ellipse to one end—is the semimajor axis, which is usually used to specify the size of the ellipse. For example, the semimajor axis of the orbit of Mars, which is also the planet's average distance from the Sun, is 228 million kilometers.

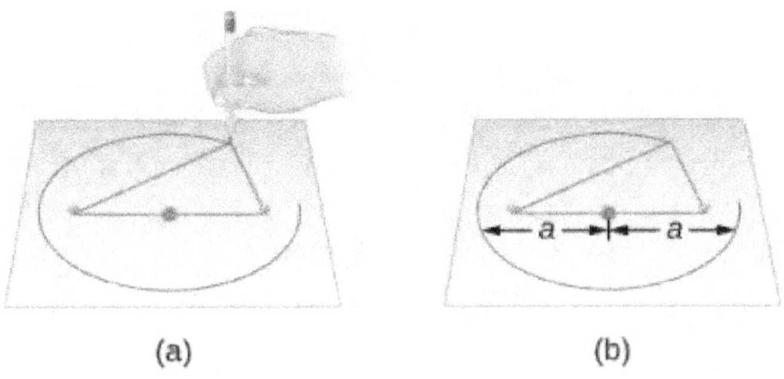

(a)   (b)

Drawing an Ellipse. (a) We can construct an ellipse by pushing two tacks (the white objects) into a piece of paper on a drawing board, and then looping a string around the tacks. Each tack represents a focus of the ellipse, with one of the tacks being the Sun. Stretch the string tight using a pencil, and then move the pencil around the tacks. The length of the string remains the same, so that the sum of the distances from any point on the ellipse to the foci is always constant. (b) In this illustration, each semimajor axis is denoted by a. The distance 2a is called the major axis of the ellipse.

The shape (roundness) of an ellipse depends on how close together the two foci are, compared with the major axis. The ratio of the distance between the foci to the length of the major axis is called the eccentricity of the ellipse. If the foci (or tacks) are moved to the same location, then the distance between the foci would be zero. This means that the eccentricity is zero and the ellipse is just a circle; thus, a circle can be called an ellipse of zero eccentricity.

In a circle, the semimajor axis would be the radius. Next, we can make ellipses of various elongations (or extended lengths) by varying the spacing of the tacks (as long as they are not farther apart than the length of the string). The greater the eccentricity, the more elongated is the ellipse, up to a maximum eccentricity of 1.0, when the ellipse becomes "flat," the other extreme from a circle. The size and shape of an ellipse are completely specified by its semimajor axis and its eccentricity.

Using Brahe's data, Kepler found that Mars has an elliptical orbit, with the Sun at one focus (the other focus is empty). The eccentricity of the orbit of Mars is only about 0.1; its orbit, drawn to scale, would be practically indistinguishable from a circle, but the difference turned out to be critical for understanding planetary motions. Kepler generalized this result in his first law and said that the orbits of all the planets are ellipses.

Here was a decisive moment in the history of human thought: it was not necessary to have only circles in order to have an acceptable cosmos. The universe could be a bit more complex than the Greek philosophers had wanted it to be.

Kepler's second law deals with the speed with which each planet moves along its ellipse, also known as its orbital speed. Working with Brahe's observations of Mars, Kepler discovered that the planet speeds up as it comes closer to the Sun and slows down as it pulls away from the Sun. He expressed the precise form of this relationship by imagining that the Sun and Mars are connected by a straight, elastic line. When Mars is closer to the Sun (positions 1 and 2 in Figure), the elastic line is not stretched as much, and the planet moves rapidly.

Farther from the Sun, as in positions 3 and 4, the line is stretched a lot, and the planet does not move so fast. As Mars travels in its elliptical orbit around the Sun, the elastic line sweeps out areas of the ellipse as it moves (the colored regions in our figure). Kepler found that in equal intervals of time (t), the areas swept out in space by this imaginary line are always equal; that is, the area of the region B from 1 to 2 is the same as that of region A from 3 to 4. If a planet moves in a circular orbit, the elastic line is always stretched the same amount and the planet moves at a constant speed around its orbit. But, as Kepler discovered, in most orbits that speed of a planet orbiting its star (or moon orbiting its planet) tends to vary because the orbit is elliptical.

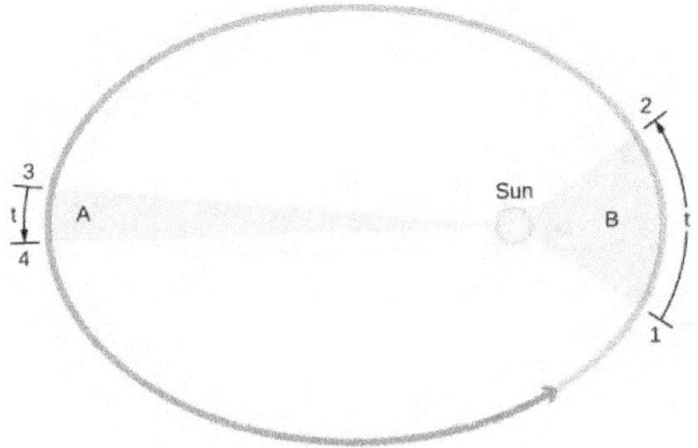

Kepler's Second Law: The Law of Equal Areas. The orbital speed of a planet traveling around the Sun (the circular object inside the ellipse) varies in such a way that in equal intervals of time (t), a line between the Sun and a planet sweeps out equal areas (A and B). Note that the eccentricities of the planets' orbits in our solar system are substantially less than shown here.

Kepler's Third Law

Kepler's first two laws of planetary motion describe the shape of a planet's orbit and allow us to calculate the speed of its motion at any point in the orbit. Kepler was pleased to have discovered such fundamental rules, but they did not satisfy his quest to fully understand planetary motions. He wanted to know why the orbits of the planets were spaced as they are and to find a mathematical pattern in their movements—a "harmony of the spheres" as he called it. For many years he worked to discover mathematical relationships governing planetary spacing and the time each planet took to go around the Sun.

In 1619, Kepler discovered a basic relationship to relate the planets' orbits to their relative distances from the Sun. We define a planet's orbital period, (P), as the time it takes a planet to travel once around the Sun. Also, recall that a planet's semimajor axis, a, is equal to its average distance from the Sun. The relationship, now known as Kepler's third law, says that a planet's orbital period squared is proportional to the semimajor axis of its orbit cubed, or

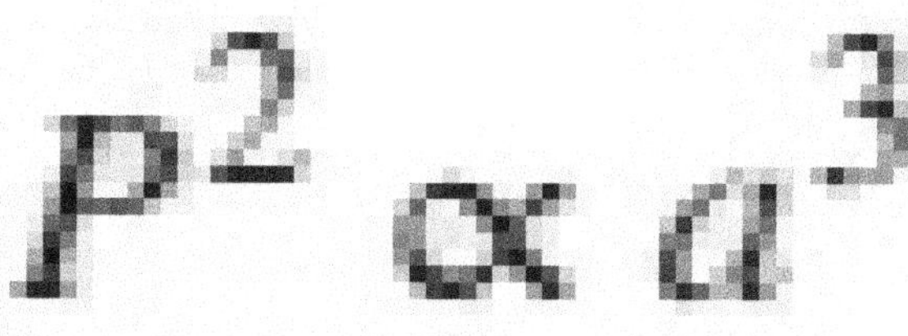

$$P^2 \propto a^3$$

When P (the orbital period) is measured in years, and a is expressed in a quantity known as an astronomical unit (AU), the two sides of the formula are not only proportional but equal. One AU is the average distance between Earth and the Sun and is approximately equal to 1.5 × 108 kilometers. In these units,

Kepler's third law applies to all objects orbiting the Sun, including Earth, and provides a means for calculating their relative distances from the Sun from the time they take to orbit. Let's look at a specific example to illustrate how useful Kepler's third law is. For instance, suppose you time how long Mars takes to go around the Sun (in Earth years).

Kepler's third law can then be used to calculate Mars' average distance from the Sun. Mars' orbital period (1.88 Earth years) squared, or

$$P^2, \text{ is } 1.88^2 = 3.53,$$

and according to the equation for Kepler's third law, this equals the cube of its semimajor axis, or a 3 . So what number must be cubed to give 3.53? The answer is 1.52 (since 1.52 × 1.52 × 1.52 = 3.53). Thus, Mars' semimajor axis in astronomical units must be 1.52 AU. In other words, to go around the Sun in a little less than two years, Mars must be about 50% (half again) as far from the Sun as Earth is.

Kepler's three laws of planetary motion can be summarized as follows:

· **Kepler's first law**: Each planet moves around the Sun in an orbit that is an ellipse, with the Sun at one focus of the ellipse.

· **Kepler's second law**: The straight line joining a planet and the Sun sweeps out equal areas in space in equal intervals of time.

· **Kepler's third law**: The square of a planet's orbital period is directly proportional to the cube of the semimajor axis of its orbit.

Kepler's three laws provide a precise geometric description of planetary motion within the framework of the Copernican system. With these tools, it was possible to calculate planetary positions with greatly improved precision. Still, Kepler's laws are purely descriptive: they do not help us understand what forces of nature constrain the planets to follow this particular set of rules. That step was left to Isaac Newton.

VI

LOCATING PLACES IN THE SKY

Positions in the sky are measured in a way that is very similar to the way we measure positions on the surface of Earth. Instead of latitude and longitude, however, astronomers use coordinates called declination and right ascension. To denote positions of objects in the sky, it is often convenient to make use of the fictitious celestial sphere.

Declination on the celestial sphere is measured the same way that latitude is measured on the sphere of Earth: from the celestial equator toward the north (positive) or south (negative). So Polaris, the star near the north celestial pole, has a declination of almost +90°. Right ascension (RA) is like longitude, except that instead of Greenwich, the arbitrarily chosen point where we start counting is the vernal equinox, a point in the sky where the ecliptic (the Sun's path) crosses the celestial equator. RA can be expressed either in units of angle (degrees) or in units of time.

This is because the celestial sphere appears to turn around Earth once a day as our planet turns on its axis. Thus the 360° of RA that it takes to go once around the celestial sphere can just as well be set equal to 24 hours. Then each 15° of arc is equal to 1 hour of time. For example, the approximate celestial coordinates of the bright star Capella are RA 5h = 75° and declination +50°. One way to visualize these circles in the sky is to imagine Earth as a transparent sphere with the terrestrial coordinates (latitude and longitude) painted on it with dark paint.

Imagine the celestial sphere around us as a giant ball, painted white on the inside. Then imagine yourself at the center of Earth, with a bright light bulb in the middle, looking out through its transparent surface to the sky. The terrestrial poles, equator, and meridians will be projected as dark shadows on the celestial sphere, giving us the system of coordinates in the sky.

The Turning Earth

Why do many stars rise and set each night? Why, in other words, does the night sky seem to turn? We have seen that the apparent rotation of the celestial sphere could be accounted for either by a daily rotation of the sky around a stationary Earth or by the rotation of Earth itself. Since the seventeenth century, it has been generally accepted that it is Earth that turns, but not until the nineteenth century did the French physicist Jean Foucault provide an unambiguous demonstration of this rotation. In 1851, he suspended a 60-meter pendulum weighing about 25 kilograms from the dome of the Pantheon in Paris and started the pendulum swinging evenly. If Earth had not been turning, there would have been no alteration of the pendulum's plane of oscillation, and so it would have continued tracing the same path. Yet after a few minutes Foucault could see that the pendulum's plane of motion was turning. Foucault explained that it was not the pendulum that was shifting, but rather Earth that was turning beneath it (Figure 4.4). You can now find such pendulums in many science centers and planetariums around the world.

Foucault's Pendulum. As Earth turns, the plane of oscillation of the Foucault pendulum shifts gradually so that over the course of 12 hours, all the targets in the circle at the edge of the wooden platform are knocked over in sequence.

The Seasons and Sunshine

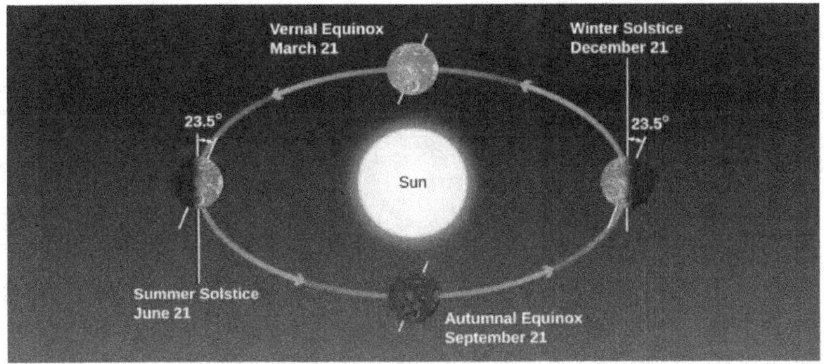

We see Earth at different seasons as it circles the Sun. In June, the Northern Hemisphere "leans into" the Sun, and those in the North experience summer and have longer days. In December, during winter in the Northern Hemisphere, the Southern Hemisphere "leans into" the Sun and is illuminated more directly. In spring and autumn, the two hemispheres receive more equal shares of sunlight.

Figure shows Earth's annual path around the Sun, with Earth's axis tilted by 23.5°. Note that our axis continues to point the same direction in the sky throughout the year. As Earth travels around the Sun, in June the Northern Hemisphere "leans into" the Sun and is more directly illuminated. In December, the situation is reversed: the Southern Hemisphere leans into the Sun, and the Northern Hemisphere leans away. In September and March, Earth leans "sideways"—neither into the Sun nor away from it—so the two hemispheres are equally favored with sunshine.

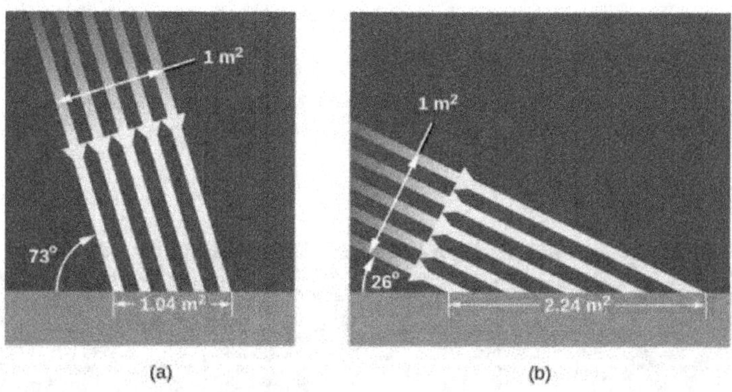

The Sun's Rays in Summer and Winter. (a) In summer, the Sun appears high in the sky and its rays hit Earth more directly, spreading out less. (b) In winter, the Sun is low in the sky and its rays spread out over a much wider area, becoming less effective at heating the ground.

How does the Sun's favoring one hemisphere translate into making it warmer for us down on the surface of Earth? There are two effects we need to consider. When we lean into the Sun, sunlight hits us at a more direct angle and is more effective at heating Earth's surface (Figure). You can get a similar effect by shining a flashlight onto a wall. If you shine the flashlight straight on, you get an intense spot of light on the wall. But if you hold the flashlight at an angle (if the wall "leans out" of the beam), then the spot of light is more spread out. Like the straight-on light, the sunlight in June is more direct and intense in the Northern Hemisphere, and hence more effective at heating.

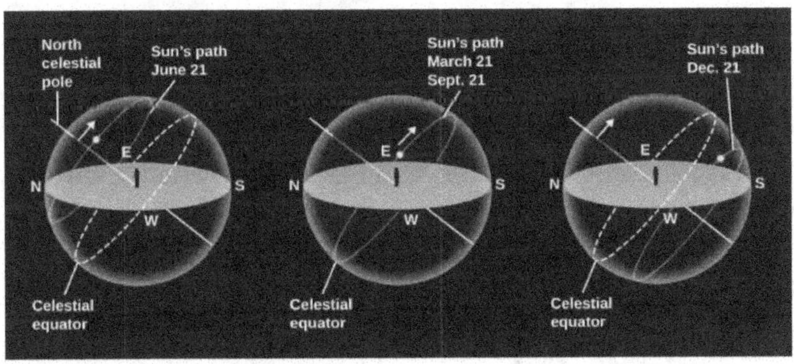

The Sun's Path in the Sky for Different Seasons. On June 21, the Sun rises north of east and sets north of west. For observers in the Northern Hemisphere of Earth, the Sun spends about 15 hours above the horizon in the United States, meaning more hours of daylight. On December 21, the Sun rises south of east and sets south of west. It spends 9 hours above the horizon in the United States, which means fewer hours of daylight and more hours of night in northern lands (and a strong need for people to hold celebrations to cheer themselves up). On March 21 and September 21, the Sun spends equal amounts of time above and below the horizon in both hemispheres.

The second effect has to do with the length of time the Sun spends above the horizon (Figure). Even if you've never thought about astronomy before, we're sure you have observed that the hours of daylight increase in summer and decrease in winter. Let's see why this happens. that the Northern Hemisphere's gain is the Southern Hemisphere's loss. There the June Sun is low in the sky, meaning fewer daylight hours. In Chile, for example, June is a colder, darker time of year.) In December, when the Sun is south of the celestial equator, the situation is reversed.

Let's look at what the Sun's illumination on Earth looks like at some specific dates of the year, when these effects are at their maximum. On or about June 21 (the date we who live in the Northern Hemisphere call the summer solstice or sometimes the first day of summer), the Sun shines down most directly upon the Northern Hemisphere of Earth. It appears about 23° north of the equator, and thus, on that date, it passes through the zenith of places on Earth that are at 23° N latitude. The situation is shown in detail in Figure. To a person at 23° N (near Hawaii, for example), the Sun is directly overhead at noon. This latitude, where the Sun can appear at the zenith at noon on the first day of summer, is called the Tropic of Cancer.

We also see in Figure that the Sun's rays shine down all around the North Pole at the solstice. As Earth turns on its axis, the North Pole is continuously illuminated by the Sun; all places within 23° of the pole have sunshine for 24 hours. The Sun is as far north on this date as it can get; thus, 90° – 23° (or 67° N) is the southernmost latitude where the Sun can be seen for a full 24-hour period (sometimes called the "land of the midnight Sun"). That circle of latitude is called the Arctic Circle.

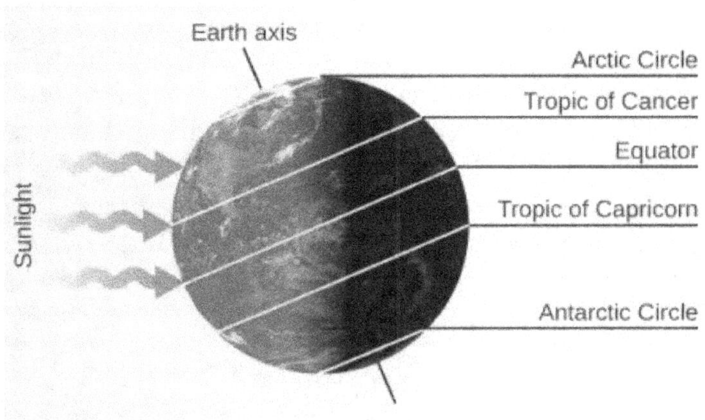

Earth on June 21. This is the date of the summer solstice in the Northern Hemisphere. Note that as Earth turns on its axis (the line connecting the North and South Poles), the North Pole is in constant sunlight while the South Pole is veiled in 24 hours of darkness. The Sun is at the zenith for observers on the Tropic of Cancer.

Many early cultures scheduled special events around the summer solstice to celebrate the longest days and thank their gods for making the weather warm. This required people to keep track of the lengths of the days and the northward trek of the Sun in order to know the right day for the "party." (You can do the same thing by watching for several weeks, from the same observation point, where the Sun rises or sets relative to a fixed landmark. In spring, the Sun will rise farther and farther north of east, and set farther and farther north of west, reaching the maximum around the summer solstice.)

Now look at the South Pole in Figure. On June 21, all places within 23° of the South Pole—that is, south of what we call the Antarctic Circle—do not see the Sun at all for 24 hours. The situation is reversed 6 months later, about December 21 (the date of the winter solstice, or the first day of winter in the Northern Hemisphere), as shown in Figure.

Now it is the Arctic Circle that has the 24-hour night and the Antarctic Circle that has the midnight Sun. At latitude 23° S, called the Tropic of Capricorn, the Sun passes through the zenith at noon. Days are longer in the Southern Hemisphere and shorter in the north. In the United States and Southern Europe, there may be only 9 or 10 hours of sunshine during the day. It is winter in the Northern Hemisphere and summer in the Southern Hemisphere.

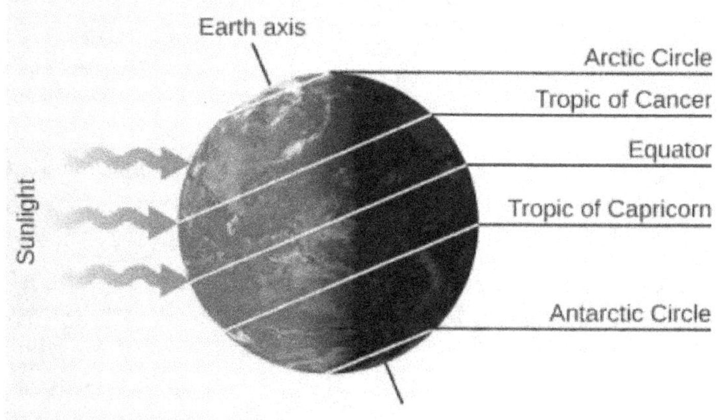

Earth on December 21. This is the date of the winter solstice in the Northern Hemisphere. Now the North Pole is in darkness for 24 hours and the South Pole is illuminated. The Sun is at the zenith for observers on the Tropic of Capricorn and thus is low in the sky for the residents of the Northern Hemisphere.

VII
ASTROLOGY IN ASTRONOMY

Indian astronomy has a long history and spans from pre-historic to modern times. Indian astronomy has earliest roots Indus Valley Civilization. Jyotish, also called Astronomy or Vedānga or one of the "auxiliary disciplines" associated with the study of the Vedas, dating about 1500 BCE or older. Vedānga Jyotisha is the oldest known text dated to 1400-1200 BCE. Indian astronomy was influenced by Greek astronomy in the 4th century BCE and through the early centuries by the Yavanajātaka and the Romaka Siddhānta, a Sanskrit translation of a Greek text. Indian astronomy flowered in the 5th–6th century, Aryabhata, an astronomer par excellence and author of Aryabhatiya, represented the pinnacle of astronomical knowledge at the time. Later the Indian astronomy was significantly elaborated on Aryabhata's work by other Indian astronomers Brahmagupta, Varāhamihira and Lalla.

Some cosmological concepts are present in the Vedas, such as the movement of heavenly bodies and the course of the year. Vedānga Jyotisha is one of the earliest known Indian texts on astronomy which includes the details about the Sun, Moon, Nakshatras, and lunisolar calendar. Later astronomers mention the existence of various siddhāntas known as 'Panchsiddhantika' and among them a text known as the Surya Siddhānta which dates to the Gupta period and was received by Aryabhata. stands tall even to date. The Pañcasiddhāntikā was due to Varāhamihira of 520AD. Hindu calendar based the divisions of the year were based on religious rites and seasons (Rtu).

The duration from mid-March to mid-May was considered to be spring (vasanta) season, midMay to mid -July: summer (grishma) season, mid-July to mid-September: rains (varsha) season, mid-September to mid-November: autumn (sharad) season, mid-Novemb to midJanuary: winter (hemanta) season, mid-January to mid-March: the dews (shishir) season. In the Vedānga Jyotiṣa, the year begins with the winter solstice. Thus, there is a close association of astronomy with Hindu religion and Hindu culture during the early development of the science. Astronomical observations are necessitated by the temple and domestic rituals for correct time of performance, failing which the results go astray and when results go astray, the world order goes astray; alas! What a great calamity is in store in the modern days of disbelief with the growing number of educated unbelievers.

Suryopanishat of Atharva Veda and Purushārthas

AUM is the sound of the infinite Brahman and the entire universe; the highest of all mantras. Aum is said to be the essence of all Vedas. In Vedas and other Hindu scriptures, Chandogya

Upanishad and Mandukya Upanishad, 'AUM' is the sound of the Sun. Recently, the Sound of AUM from the Sun was recorded by NASA. AUM is the sound of the Sun, the sound of Light and uplifts the soul. The Solar family is symbolical of the four 'Purushārthas' for fulfilment of worldly life. It is mentioned in Suryopanishat of Atharva Veda that Sun God bestows on us the four Purushārthas.

ॐम्अथ सूर्याथर्र्याङ्गरिसं व्ययख्ययस्ययमः । ब्रह्मय ड्ङ्गष: । गयर्त्री छन्द: ।

आङ्गत्यियो र्तिय । हंशः सोऽहमड्ङ्गनियर्रयरर्णर्कृतम्बीजम । हृड्ङ्लेख्य शक्क्त: । ड्गर्र्र्यिङ्गसिगाकीलकम । चतड्ङ्गर्राधपुरुषयथाङ्गसयिथेड्ङ्गर्ड्ङ्गनरोग: ।

---Suryopanishat of Atharva Veda

Om˜ atha sūryātharvāṅgirasaṃ vyākhyāsyāmaḥ ı brahmā ṛṣiḥ ı gāyatrī chandaḥ ı ādityo devatā ı haṃsaḥ

The counterpart of the Sun, Mercury, Ketu and Venus areSaturn, Jupiter, Rāhu and Mars respectively. Further, a striking fact emerges out that these planets could combine as a pair consisting of one planet from the Interior Group and one from the Exterior Group with similar and parallel qualities. These pairs are:

i) The Sun-Saturn

ii) Mercury-Jupiter

iii) Rāhu and Ketu

iv) Venus-Mars

v) Earth and Moon.

Thus, these pairs signify Moksha, Dharma, Māya, Artha and Kāma respectively. In between lies Rāhu-Ketu evil axis which veils knowledge and deludes the soul. It is 'Maya'. Its nature is explained in Bhagavad Gita as follows:

so'hamagninārāyaṇayuktaṃ   bījam   ı   hṛllekhā   śaktiḥ ıviyadādisargasaṃyuktaṃ   kīlakam   ı caturvidhapuruṣārthasiddhyarthe viniyogaḥ ı

Solar System and Purushārthas

The Vedas envisage four objectives viz. Dharma, Artha, Kāma and Moksha for human beings to find fulfillment in worldly life. The very term "Purushārtha" used to refer to them gives the insight that their pursuit makes human life meaningful. Two of them Kāma and Artha relate to worldly life and they are desire and materialistic ends. The other two are Dharma and Moksha (liberation from rebirths i.e. selfrealisation). The Solar family symbolises the four 'Purushārthas' for fulfilment of worldly life. The intricacies of the planetary nature reveal that every planet of the Interior Group has a counterpart from the Exterior Group with similar and parallel qualities and form the four purushārthas besides the evil axis 'māya'

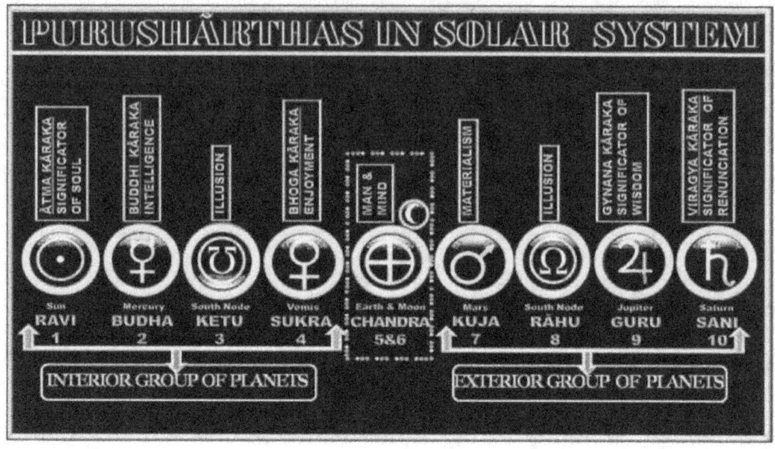

Interior and Exterior Groups of Planets of Solar System with their Astrological Significations

धूमेनयङ्गरि्ते रृ्ङ्गरिथयशो मलेन च | र्थोल्बनेयरृ्तो गरा्स्तथय तेनेमियरृ्तम् ॥ 38॥

---Bhagavad Gita Chapter 3, Verse 38

dhūmenāvriyate vahnir yathādarśho malena cha yatholbenāvṛito garbhas tathā tenedam āvṛitam

Translation: Just as a fire is covered by smoke, a mirror is masked by dust, and an embryo is concealed by the womb, similarly one's knowledge gets shrouded by desire. This axis is also related to the tiny sleeping coiled serpent (Rajju-Sarpa Nyāyam) and this is to be awakened and raised to the pineal gland in the brain (Sahasrāra Chakra) when 'Māya' vanishes to realize the Ātman, through Dharma

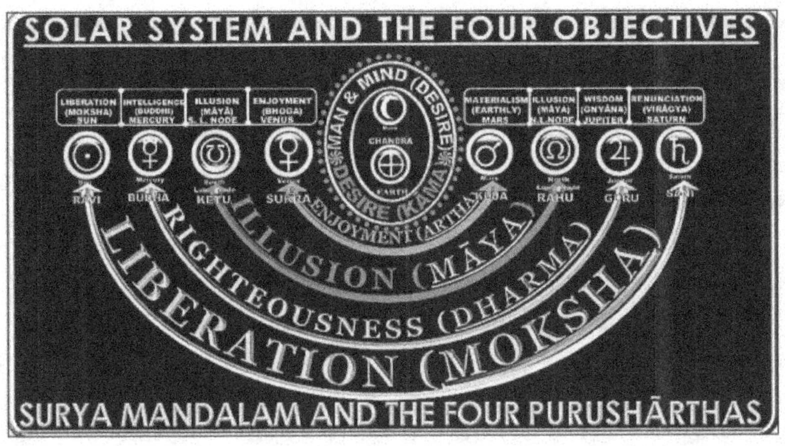

Planets of Solar System with their Astrological Significations signifying the four Purushārthas and the evil axis 'Māya'

Sankalpam and Sandhyāvandanam

"Sankalpam" is a prayer to God and Saints informing the individual's identity, location in the Universe and time for their blessings. We owe our forefathers for carrying on the legacy for the benefit of posterity.

The name of the present Kalpa is Sweta Varāha Kalpa. In the present Kalpa, six Manvantaras plus Sandhis have been completed and the seventh Manvantara by name Vaivasvata Manvantara is running. In this Manvantara, 27 Mahā Yugas have passed and we are in the twenty-eighth (28) Mahā Yuga. In this 28th Mahā Yuga, three Yugas have passed and the fourth, that is Kali Yuga's first quarter started about 4670 years ago.

This is the reason that before commencing any Puja, Ritual or Vratam (Worship), we start invoking the Gods, reminding ourselves of the time elapsed to date since the existence of the universe to the time of performance, the coordinates of the place of performance, the lineage of the performer by chanting the Sankalpa thus:

Adya Brahmanaha l Dwiteeya Parardhey l Sri Sweta Varāha Kalpey l Vaivaswata Manvantarey l Kali Yugey l Prathama Pādey l Jamboo Dweepey l Bharata Varshey l Bharata Khandey l Meror l Dakshina Digbhāgey l Sri Sailasya Āgneya Pradesey l Krishna-Kāveryor Madhya Desey l Samastha Devatā Brāhmana Sannidhou l Asmin l Vartamāna Vyāvahārika Chāndra Mānena l Vikarināma Samvatsarey l

Uttarāyaney l Sisira Ritau l Phalguna Māsey l Sukla Pakshey l Vidiya Thithou l Mangala Vāsarayukthāyām l Purvābhadra Nakshatrey l Trāyarsheya Āngirasa, Bāryhaspatya, Bhāradwāja Gotram l 6000 Sākhādyāyee l Subba Rāo Sarmānām l Sandhyāvandanam upasishye l. In the "sankalpam" reference is made to 'Time' to the present existence of the universe up to pronouncing 'Pradhama Pādhe'; next, reference is made to place; Finally, it is followed by the Individual's identity. What an uncanny ability of ancient Hindus in the Way of Time and Geotagging of "Sankalpam" to Cosmos!

Rationale of Names of Days of the Week

The Week Days are named after their Lords (Planets). The successive fifth in the ascending order of distances in the Geocentric Model is the successive Lord of the Day beginning with the Moon; the Moon always starts the time orders. All Time Orders in Astronomy are reckoned from the Moon as its angular motion is $13\frac{1}{3}0$ degrees per day is the criterion. Thus, the successive Lords of the Days of the week are reckoned from the Moon [2] . To Moon (denoting Monday), Mars (denoting Tuesday) is the fifth. Similarly, to Mars (Tuesday), Mercury (denoting Wednesday) is the fifth, and so on

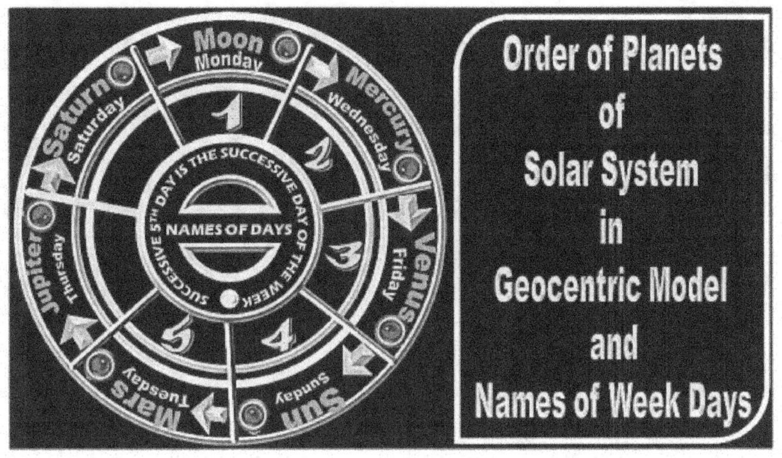

Sequence of Days of the Week

Rāhukālam Timings and Sequence of Rāhukālam Days of Week

Within any given day, there is a certain time period that is inauspicious known as Rāhukālam. The Siddhas say that it is ideal to use these periods for spiritual activity and not use for material activities signified by 4th house from Lagna in Astrology. If these time periods are used for worship and not for material activities, they yield manifold spiritual benefits.

The successive Lords of the Month;

ii. The successive Lords of the Days;

iii. The successive Lords of the Year;

iv. The successive Lords of Rāhukālam; and

v. The successive planetary periods (Dasās)

In Astrology are all reckoned from the Moon. Thus, the successive 4th Lords from the Moon in the Solar System are the Rāhukālam Times' Lords. To Moon (denoting Monday) Saturn (denoting Saturday) is the fourth. Similarly, to Saturn (denoting Saturday), Venus (denoting Friday) is the fourth, and so on Further, the 4th house signifies material prosperity in Astrology, material

activities are prohibited during these

Sequence of Rāhukālam Times on the Seven Days of the Week

The time period between Sunrise and Sunset is divided into eight equal parts, which are referred to as time octants. The Rāhukālam Days of the Week are arranged in the order Monday, Saturday, Friday, Wednesday, Thursday, Tuesday, Sunday. The second through the eighth-time octants is assigned to these Days in this order as the Days are only Seven. These time octants then are the Rāhukālam times on each of the Days of the Week

times as Rāhu chooses the successive 4th Lords for destroying material activity. It can also be observed that there exists an error in the sequence of conventional observation of 'Rāhukālam Days' of Wednesday and Thursday. The correct sequence is that Rāhukālam Day is Thursday immediately after Friday and Wednesday is next to Thursday. That this is correct is evidenced by the fact that the sequence of Rāhukālam days are in the retrograde order, viz., Saturday, Friday, Thursday, Wednesday, Tuesday, Sunday, Monday

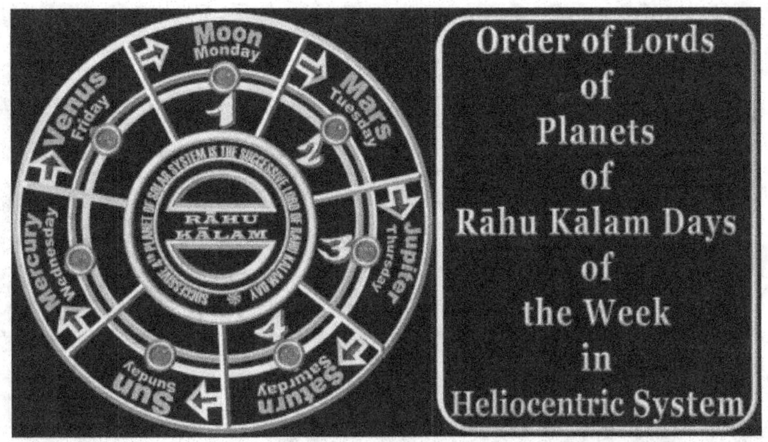

Sequence of Rāhukālam Days of the Week

Rationale of Hindu Gothras

In astronomy, Saptarishi Mandalam is known as 'Ursa Major or Big Bear'. It is Bear because the seven stars of Saptarishi Mandalam with other neighbouring stars resemble a Bear. It is 'Big' because another cluster similar to and mirror image of it just above it is called 'Ursa Minor' or 'Little Bear' wherein Polaris is a star in line with Merak and Dubhe stars (Figure). The word gotra means "lineage" in the Sanskrit language. In Hindu society, the term gotra (Sanskrit: गोत्र) means clan. It broadly refers to people who are descendants in an unbroken male line from a common male ancestor or patrilineal of Saptarishis. People with same gotra are considered to be siblings. The classification of gotra came into existence in Vedic period. This Gotra custom was established to avoid marriages between blood relatives. Marriages within the same gotra ('sagotra') marriages are not permitted in the traditional matrimonial system. This custom was established to avoid marriages between blood relatives in the backdrop of more abnormalities in children born to sagotra couple. Modern genetics corroborate this view point

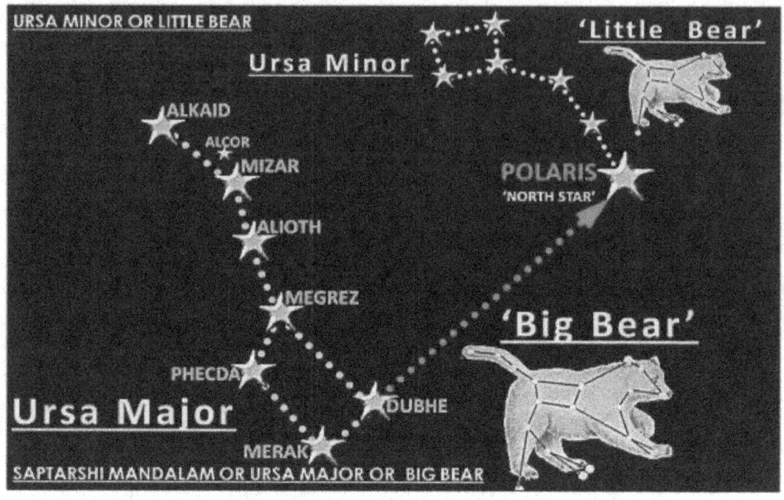

Saptarshi Mandalam (Ursa Major) and Polaris (Ursa Minor)

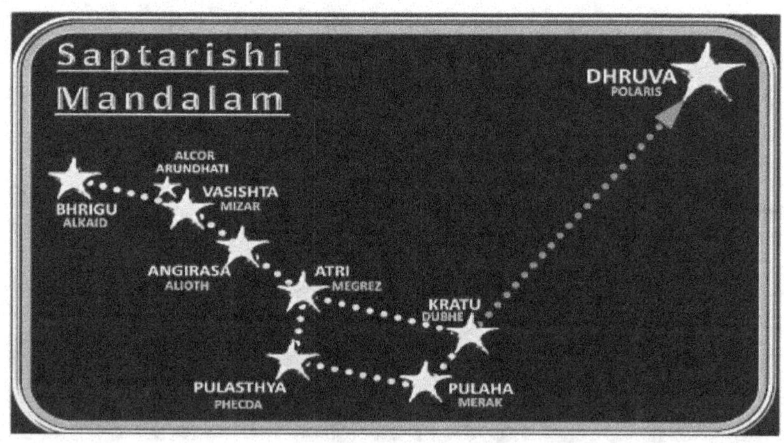

Saptarshi Mandalam (Ursa Major and Ursa Minor)

Rationale of Significance of Viewing Mizar, Alcor and Polaris Stars by the Newly Married Couple

In one of the rituals of a Hindu Marriage, the couple are asked to look up for Arundhati (Alcor) and Vasishta (Mizar), an ideal couple, in the Saptarishi Constellation. These twin stars are Binary stars and rotate in synchrony symbolizing conjugal love and affection and to tell that both husband and wife must do all things in synchronisation. The couple are also to look up for Dhruva, the Pole Star as it carries a greater significance of married life. This Saptarishi Constellation, comprising Arundhati and Vasishta, in Northern Hemisphere appears to rotate around the pole star 'Dhruva' or Polaris. Newly wedded bride views Dhruva for Stability in the in-law's house Both Bride and Groom view Arundhati for Chastity and Celibacy; both the Bride and Groom view Vasishta for carrying on Family Legacy

'Shashti Abda Poorthi'

'Shashti Abda Poorthi' in Sanskrit means sixty years completion; 'Shashti' means 60, 'Abda' means years, and'Poorthi' means completion. It is also known as'Shashti Poorthi'. It is a ceremony celebrated to commemorate completion of 60 years of age of the male. It marks completion of half the years of one's lifetime as in Hindu Religion, 120 years is considered the life span of a human being. The sages and the rishis of lore have acknowledged the sanctity of the sixtieth year in one's life and have drawn out elaborate rituals to mark this special event. This point of life is a sacred part of the hallowed Vedic culture. The Hindu Calendar has 60 years (named Prabhava, Vibhava, etc. upto Kshayanāma Samvatsara) that repeat themselves after every 60 years in a sequence. Shashti Poorthi marks the completion of one such cycle. In a hundred and twenty-year time scale of man's life, pre-sixty is a period of materialistic pursuit while the post-sixty span is slated for spiritual endeavour. Another circumstance or practice may be referred to in connection with the total of the planetary period of 120 years. There is clearly a connection between the motion of the Moon through the 360 degrees of the Zodiac, of the planetary periods of 120 years thrice over and Poorna Ãyurdãya of 120 years. Vedic Astrology considers the age of 60 years as Madhya Ãyurdãya.

'Sathãbhishekham'

The revolution periods of Jupiter and Saturn are 12 and 30 years respectively. Assuming both the planets Jupiter and Saturn are originally in Aries, they both return to the same sign Aries after completing 5 revolutions and 2 revolutions respectively. In Hindu Religion, 'Sathãbhishekham' ceremony is performed by the family members on the completion of 80 years by the man 20 years after Shasti Poorti when we find Jupiter meets Saturn in the sign Scorpio (the 8th sign from Aries) (Figure). The couple is considered

Jupiter and Saturn for 'Shastyabdapoorti' and 'Satabhishekham'

It is explained that a person having completed the age of 80 years, 8 months and 8 days would have passed through 1000 moons, 'Sathãbhishekham' is done. (1000 X 29.53)/ 365.25 = 80.8 years. Saint Vaikãnasa feels 80 years and 8 months are sufficient enough for 'Sathãbhishekham'. Interestingly enough, in Vedic Astrology the 8th house signifies longevity.

Rationale and Significance of Uttarāyana (Winter Solstice) and Dakshināyana (Summer Solstice)

Uttarāyana (Winter Solstice) always occurs on the 22nd December and Dakshināyana (Summer Solstice) always occurs on the 22nd June and in between the two, we have

'Ichha mrityu' of Grandsire Bhishma Uttarāyaṇa (उत्तरयर्ण)

consists of Sanskrit words "Uttara" (North) and "āyana" (movement) means the northward journey of the Sun or the Winter Solstice. Uttarāyana starts when Sun enters into Capricorn in the Zodiac on the 21-22 Dec., this moment is called Uttarāyana Punyakāla which all to have crossed 1000 full moons in their lifetime and get the blessings of Moon. This is the time to increase the spirituality and aspire for Moksha

Spring Equinox occurring on the 21st March and Autumn Equinox occurring on the 23rd September each year.

These are the four cardinal points of the Zodiac and four quarters of a Year which are beyond any controversy (Figure). But in India, all the spiritual and religious activities in Hindu Religion take place during the Sun centric period Uttarāyana Punyakāla (Makara Samkramana) which is religiously observed on the 13th or the 14th, January nearly three weeks after its actual occurrence. However, the Sun is not prepared to wait for the Panchāng (Indian Almanac) to come into line. In Dwapara Yuga, Ugadi always occurs with the beginning of Winter Solstice i.e., on December 21st.

Hindus consider holy and celestial. This period is also referred to as Devayāna (with the Gods being placed at the North Pole). The doors of Vaikuntam, (Moksha Dwāram), the abode of Supreme Lord Sri Mahā Vishnu are opened on the day of advent of Uttarāyana. It is the belief of every Hindu that those who die during the six months' period of

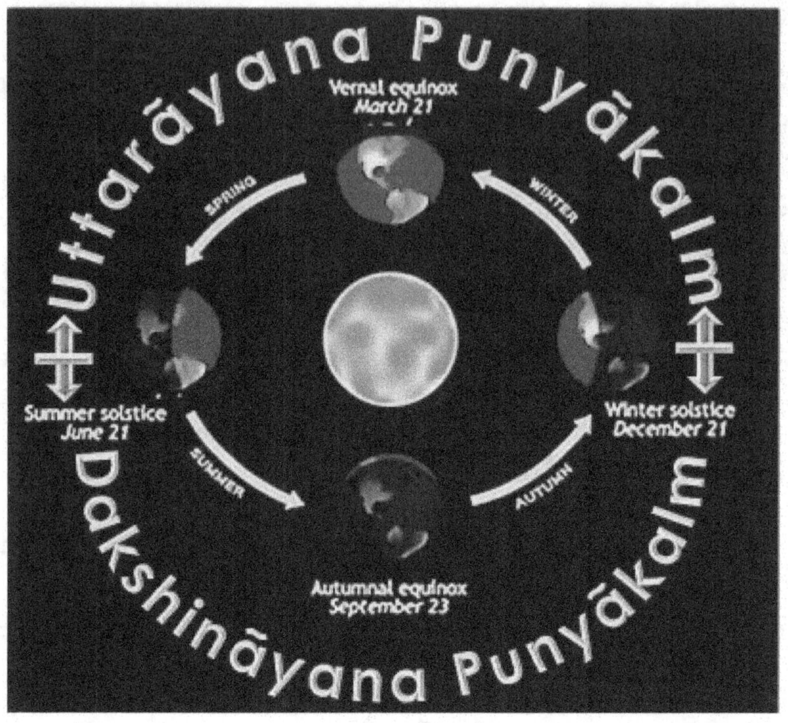

The Four Cardinal Points two equinoxes and two solstices of the Zodiac and Four Quarters of the Astronomical Year

Uttarāyana will attain salvation (Moksha). During the Mahābhārat War, Bhishma Pitāmaha fell from his chariot on the 10th day. His body did not touch the ground. It was kept aloft on the bed of protruding arrows pierced into his body in the war. Grandsire Bhishma expressed his intent to wait for 58 days when Uttarāyana starts (Figure). Bhishma was waiting for the advent of Uttarāyana punyakālam (winter solstice). he had the boon to die at will called 'Ichha mrityu' or 'Swatchanda Maranam' granted by his father. Bhishma waited for 58 days on his death bed for the onset of Uttarāyana.

Dakshināyana (Winter Solstice)

Dakshinayana (Sanskrit: ड्रिगणियर्ण) is the six-month period between Summer Solstice and Winter Solstice, when the Sun travels towards the south on the celestial sphere. Dakshinayana marks the transition of the Sun into Karka Rāsi (Cancer). According to the Purānas, Dakshinayana marks the period when the gods and goddesses are in their celestial sleep. Dakshinayana is defined as the period between the Autumnal and Vernal Equinoxes, when there is midnight sun at the South Pole. This period is also referred to as Pitrayāna (with the Pitrus (i.e. ancestors) being placed at the South Pole). Dakshinayana is significant in the life of anyone who is doing any kind of yoga. Uttarāyana is considered the daytime of the Gods residing at the North Pole which tradition makes sense only if we define Uttarāyana as the period between the Vernal and Autumnal equinoxes (when there is Midnight Sun at the North Pole).

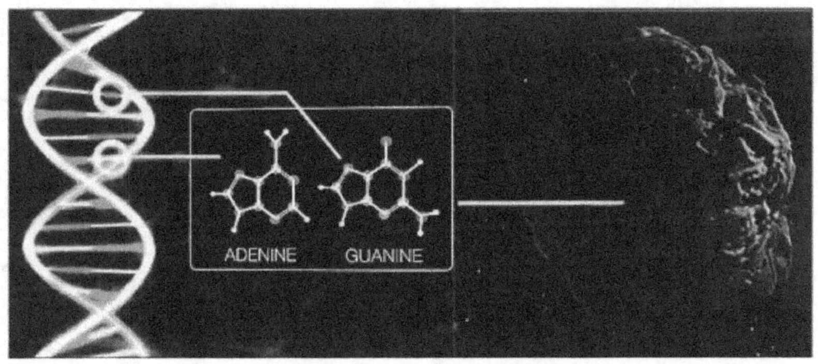

NASA found DNA Building Blocks in Meteorites likely created in space

Later, it was also mentioned that these life building blocks found by them were intact despite the heavy re-entry temperature of meteorites about 1650 degrees Centigrade when they hit the earth's atmosphere. The amino acids did not break down due to heat and shock of the simulated crash is possibly due to the invisible and indestructible shield called spirit or Soul enveloping them vide Bhagavad Gita.

Conversely, Dakshināyana is defined as the period between the Autumnal and Vernal Equinoxes, when there is midnight Sun at the South Pole. This period is also referred to as Pitrayāna (with the Pitrus (i.e. ancestors) being placed at the South Pole). Like Rāhukalam, during Dakshināyana, spiritual practices should be concentrated upon for attaining liberation or Moksha from the birth-death cycle.

Pitrayāna and Devayāna: The Two Paths of Journey of the Soul

An enlightened person attains liberation or Moksha and never returns. There is no rebirth for him. His soul takes the path of Devayāna whereas the soul of a sinner takes the other route 'Pitrayāna'. Thus, it is said a "Saint has a Past" and a "Sinner has a Future" for the former returns not for he attained Moksha while the latter returns to take birth as defined in Bhagavad Gita.

शुक्लकृ ष्णेगती ह्यैतेजगतः शाश्वतमेतो एकया यात्यनावृततमिन्ययावततततेपुनः ॥८-२६॥

Bhagavad Gita Ch.8 – Verse26

sukla-krsne gati hy ete jagatah sāsvate mate। ekayā yāti anāvrttim anyayāvartate punah॥

Meaning: These two paths of the world, the bright and the dark, are considered to be eternal; by one, one returns not, and by the other, one returns.

Meteorites

A meteoroid is a sand- to boulder-sized particle of debris in the Solar System which collides with the Earth. The visible path of a meteoroid that enters Earth's (or another body's) atmosphere is called a meteor, or colloquially a shooting star or falling star. If a meteoroid reaches the ground and survives impact, then it is called a meteorite [9]. Astrobiology Division of NASA stated that life building blocks of DNA are found in meteorites brought to the Earth by them vide Bhagav Gita.

नैनं छिन्दन्ति शस्त्राणि नैनं दहति पावकः |
न चैनं क्लेदयन्त्यापो न शोषयति मारुतः || 23||

nainaṁ chhindanti śhastrāṇi nainaṁ dahati pāvakaḥ
na chainaṁ kledayantyāpo na śhoṣhayati mārutaḥ
--- Vide the Bhagavad Gita: Chapter2 Verse 23

VIII
THE ATMOSPHERIC FILTER

Earth's atmosphere is essential to life. This ocean of fluids and suspended particles surrounds Earth and protects it from the hazards of outer space. It insulates the inhabitants of Earth from the extreme temperatures of space and stops all but the larger meteoroids from reaching the surface. Furthermore, it filters out most radiation dangerous to life. Without the atmosphere, life would not be possible on Earth. The atmosphere contains the oxygen we breathe. It also has enough pressure so that water remains liquid at moderate temperatures.

Yet the same atmosphere that makes life possible hinders our understanding of Earth's place in the universe. Our only means for investigating distant stars, nebulae, and galaxies is to collect and analyze the electromagnetic radiation these objects emit into space. However, most of this radiation is absorbed or distorted by the atmosphere before it can reach a ground-based telescope. Only visible light and some radio waves, infrared, and ultraviolet light survive the passage from space to the ground. That limited amount of radiation has provided astronomers enough information to estimate the general shape and size of the universe and categorize its basic components, but there is much left to learn.

It is essential to study the entire spectrum rather than just limited regions of it. Relying only on the radiation that reaches Earth's surface is like listening to a piano recital on a piano that has just a few of its keys working.

Unit Goal

• To demonstrate how the components of Earth's atmosphere absorb or distort incoming electromagnetic radiation.

Teaching Strategy

The following demonstrations are designed to show how components of Earth's atmosphere filter or distort electromagnetic radiation. Since we cannot produce all of the different wavelengths of electromagnetic radiation in a classroom, the light from a slide or overhead projector in a darkened room will represent the complete electromagnetic spectrum. A projection screen will represent Earth's surface and objects placed between the projector and the screen will represent various components of Earth's atmosphere. All of the demonstrations can be conducted in a single class period. Place the projector in the back of the classroom and aim it towards the screen at the front. Try to get the room as dark as possible before doing the demonstrations.

ACTIVITY: Clear Air

Description:

Students observe some of the problems inherent in using astronomical telescopes on Earth's surface through a series of brief demonstrations given by the teacher.

Objectives:

To demonstrate how Earth's atmosphere interferes with the passage of electromagnetic radiation.

National Education Standards: Science Evidence, models, & explanation Transfer of energy Technology Understand troubleshooting, R & D, invention, innovation, & experimentation

Materials and Tools: For all demonstrations Darkened room Overhead or slide projector Worksheet for each student

• Demonstration 1 Small sheet of clear glass or Plexiglass™ Emery paper (fine) to smooth sharp edges of glass or plastic

• Demonstration 2 Shallow dish or pie tin Empty coffee can Ice Spray bottle and water Cloud cutout (cardboard or other material)

• Demonstration 3 Stick matches Eye protection

• Demonstration 4 Food warmer fuel (e.g. Sterno™) or electric hotplate Matches if using fuel Eye protection if using fuel Aluminum foil Sewing pin

• Demonstration 5 150 to 200 watt light bulb Uncovered light fixture Star slide (see demonstration 4)

Background:

Earth's atmosphere appears to be clear to the naked eye. On a dark, cloud-free night far from city lights, thousands of stars are visible. It is hard to imagine a better view of the sky when the wisps of the Milky Way Galaxy are visible stretching from the northern to the southern sky. In spite of the apparent clarity, the view is flawed. Many wavelengths are blocked by the atmosphere and visible light is filtered and distorted.

The demonstrations that follow are designed to show how Earth's atmosphere interferes with the passage of electromagnetic radiation. Visible light is used as an example of all wavelengths since most other wavelengths of electromagnetic radiation are difficult and even dangerous to produce in the classroom. Make sure students understand that the demonstrations are examples of what happens across the entire electromagnetic spectrum.

Management and Tips:

To make effective use of the demonstrations, it is necessary to have a room that can be darkened. A projection screen will represent Earth's surface and the light cast by an overhead or slide projector will represent all the wavelengths of electromagnetic radiation coming to Earth from space. The demonstrations are things that you do between the screen and the projector to represent phenomena occurring in Earth's atmosphere.

The actual demonstrations will take approximately 15 minutes to complete. Allow time to discuss the significance of each demonstration with your students. The most important thing to know is that Earth's atmosphere only allows a small portion of the electromagnetic spectrum to reach Earth's surface and astronomers' telescopes. The information astronomers can collect is incomplete and thus the story of the universe they are able to construct from this information is also incomplete. Conclude the discussion with the question "What can astronomers do about it?" The answer is to move observatories off the surface of Earth into outer space.

Procedures:

Demonstration 1 – The Air Is Not Clear

In this demonstration you will hold up a sheet of "clear" glass between the projector and screen. The glass represents the gases in Earth's atmosphere. Light from the projector is interrupted by the glass in its passage to the screen. Notice the faint shadow the "clear" glass casts on the screen. The shadow is evidence of a small amount of absorption of light by the glass. Also look for a reflection from the glass back in the direction of space. Photographs of Earth from space show a thin bluish layer of gas surrounding Earth. Being able to see the atmosphere from space indicates that some of the electromagnetic radiation falling on it from space is reflected back out into space.

Demonstration 2 – Water in the Air

To begin this demonstration, fill a coffee can with ice cubes. The can is set in the middle of a dish or pie tin and left undisturbed. In a few minutes, the

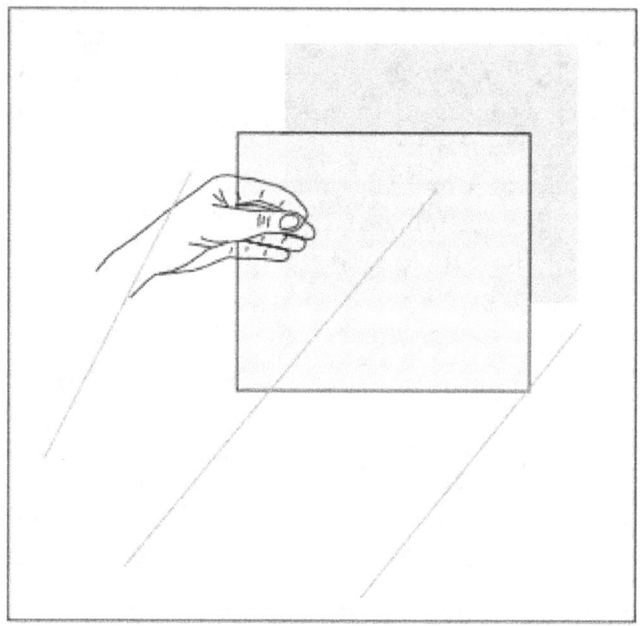

outer surface of the can will begin "sweating." This is evidence that the air in the classroom holds moisture that condenses out when it comes in contact with a cold surface.

In the second part of the demonstration, spray a fine mist of water in the air between the projector and the screen. This illustrates how fine water droplets suspended in the air will block electromagnetic radiation. High humidity casts a haze in the sky that blocks incoming visible light.

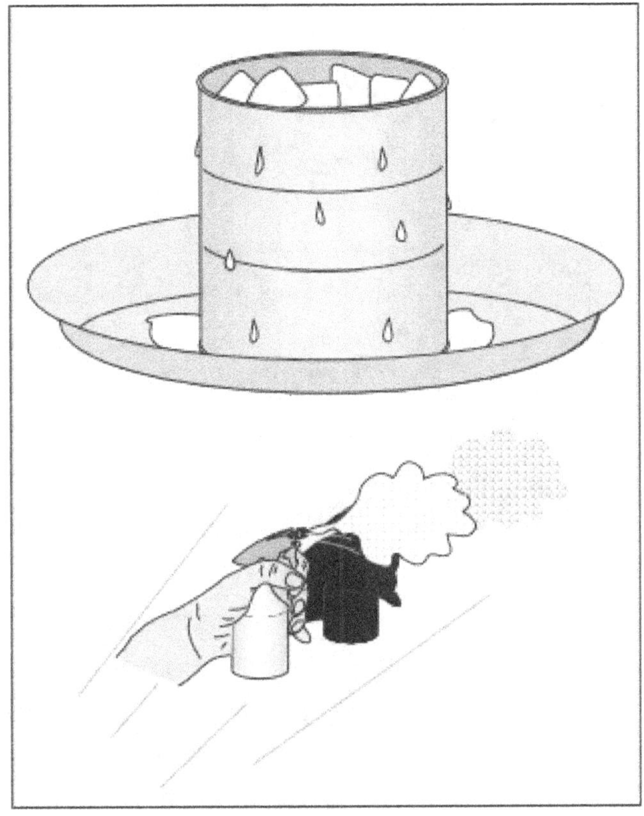

Finally, hold up the cloud cutout. The cloud shows what happens when moisture condenses in the air around small dust particles. The shadow cast by the cloud shows how clouds can substantially block visible light coming to Earth from space.

Demonstration 3 – Pollution

While wearing eye protection, strike a match and then blow it out right away. The smoke particles released from the match head will produce a noticeable shadow on the screen. Pollution from a variety of sources (human-made and natural) block some of the incoming visible light.

Demonstration 4 – Heat Currents

Prior to the demonstration, create a star slide. If you are using a slide projector, obtain a plastic slide mount in which the film can be removed. Slip a small square of aluminum foil into the

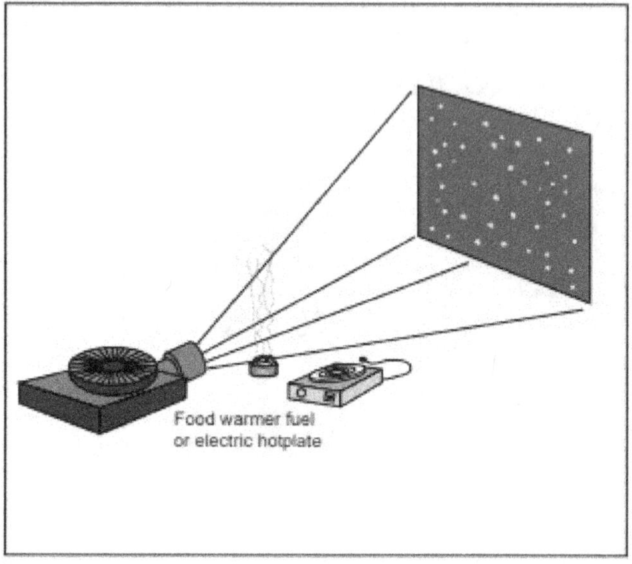

slide frame and use a pin to randomly prick about 30 holes into the foil. If you are using an overhead projector, prepare a star slide from a large square of aluminum foil. The square should cover the entire stage of the projector. Poke about 100 holes through the foil.

Project light through the slide you prepared. A small star field will be displayed on the screen. While wearing eye protection (not necessary if using an electric hot plate), place the warmer very near and just below the beam of the projector. Stars will show a twinkling effect on the screen. This demonstration shows how heat currents in Earth's atmosphere can distort the images of astronomical objects.

Demonstration 5 – Day/Night
Use the star slide you prepared in the previous activity. Hold up the lamp with the light bulb

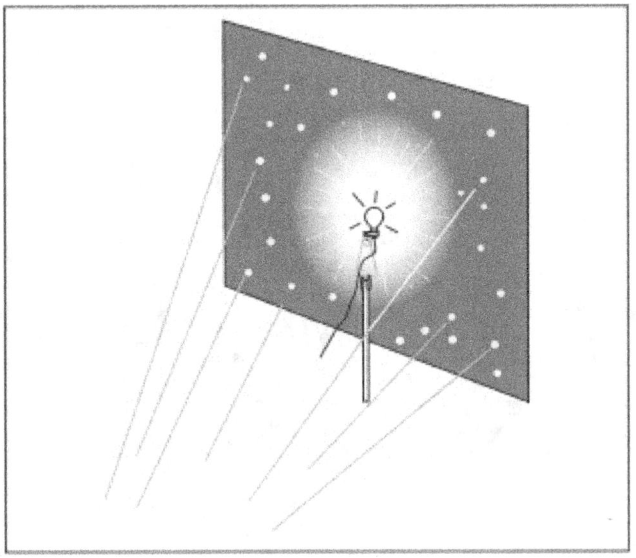

near the screen. Turn on the bulb. Many of the stars on the screen near the bulb will disappear. This demonstration shows how the Sun's light overpowers the fainter stars. Sunlight brightens the gases, water, and particles in Earth's atmosphere so that the distant stars are not visible. If the Sun's light could be dimmed, other stars would be visible at the same time.

IX

THE ELECTROMAGNETIC SPECTRUM

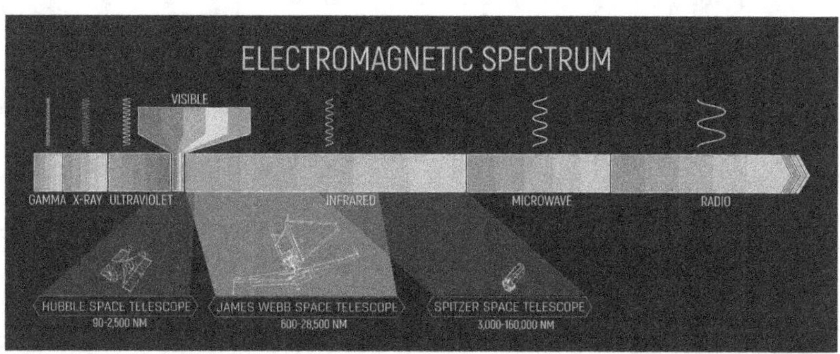

Contrary to popular belief, outer space is not empty space. It is filled with electromagnetic radiation that crisscrosses the universe. This radiation comprises the spectrum of energy ranging from radio waves on one end to gamma rays on the other. It is called the electromagnetic spectrum because this radiation is associated with electric and magnetic fields that transfer energy as they travel through space. Because humans can see it, the most familiar part of the electromagnetic spectrum is visible light—red, orange, yellow, green, blue, and violet.

Like expanding ripples in a pond after a pebble has been tossed in, electromagnetic radiation travels across space in the form of waves. These waves travel at the speed of light—300,000 kilometers per second. Their wavelengths, the distance from wave crest to wave crest, vary from thousands of kilometers across (in the case of the longest radio waves) to fractions of a nanometer, in the cases of the smallest x-rays and gamma rays.

Electromagnetic radiation has properties of both waves and particles. What we detect depends on the method we use to study it. The beautiful colors that appear in a soap film or in the dispersion of light from a diamond are best described as waves. The light that strikes a solar cell to produce an electric current is best described as a particle. When described as particles, individual packets of electromagnetic energy are called photons. The amount of energy a photon of light contains depends upon its wavelength. Electromagnetic radiation with long billionth. Thus 700 nanometers is a distance equal to 700 billionths or 7×10^{-7} meter.) Visible light is a very narrow band of radiation ranging from 400 to 700 nanometers. For comparison, it would take 50 visible light waves arranged end to end to span the thickness of a sheet of household plastic wrap. Below visible light is the slightly broader band of ultraviolet light that lies between 10 and 300 nanometers. X-rays follow ultraviolet light and diminish into the hundred-billionth of a meter range. Gamma rays fall in the trillionth of a meter range.

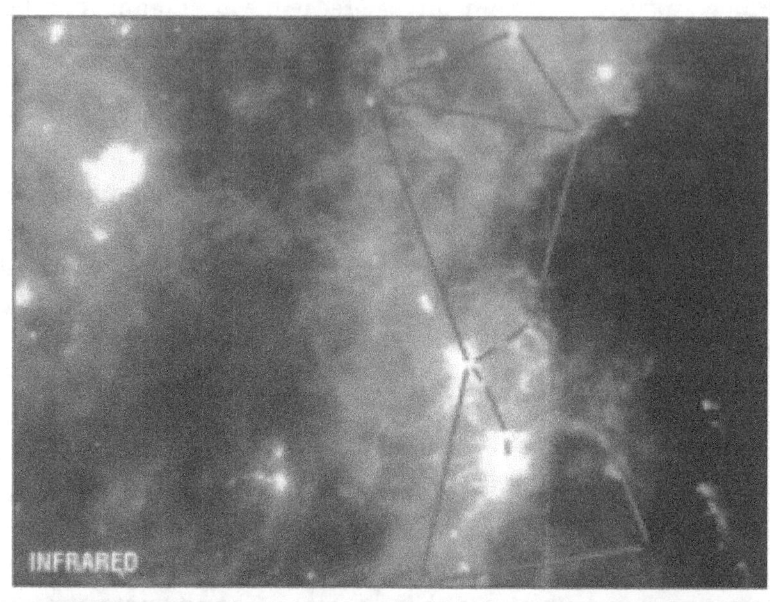
INFRARED

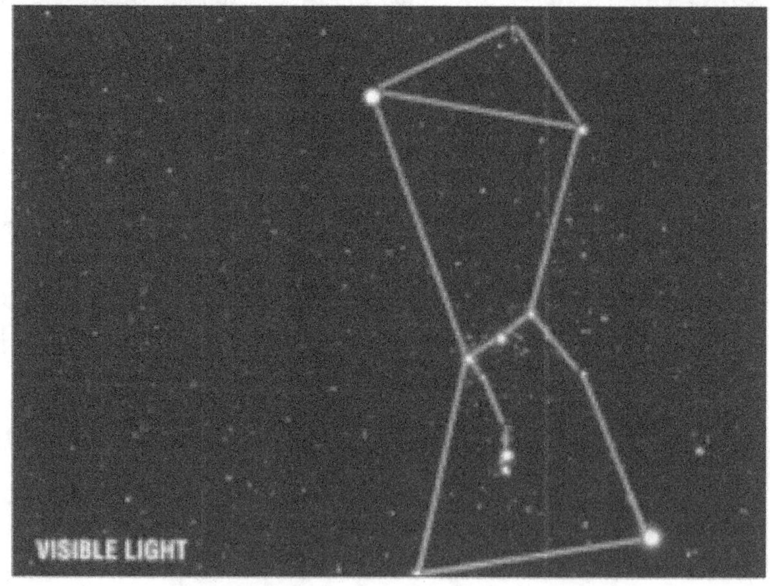
VISIBLE LIGHT

These two views of the constellation Orion dramatically illustrate the difference between what we are able to detect in visible light from Earth's surface and what is detectable in infrared light to a spacecraft in Earth orbit. Photo

The wavelengths of x-rays and gamma rays are so tiny that scientists use another unit, the electron volt, to describe them. This is the energy that an electron gains when it falls through a potential difference, or voltage, of one volt. It works out that one electron volt has a wavelength of about 0.0001 centimeters. X-rays range from 100 electron volts (100 eV) to thousands of electron volts. Gamma rays range from thousands of electron volts to billions of electron volts.

Using the Electromagnetic Spectrum

All objects in space are very distant and difficult for humans to visit. Only the Moon has been visited so far. Instead of visiting stars and planets, astronomers collect electromagnetic radiation from them using a variety of tools. Radio dishes capture radio signals from space. Big telescopes on Earth gather visible and infrared light. Interplanetary spacecraft have traveled to all the planets in our solar system except Pluto and have landed on two. No spacecraft has ever brought back planetary material for study. They send back all their information by radio waves.

Virtually everything astronomers have learned about the universe beyond Earth depends on the information contained in the electromagnetic radiation that has traveled to Earth. For example, when a star explodes as in a supernova, it emits energy in all wavelengths of the electromagnetic spectrum. The most famous supernova is the stellar explosion that became visible in 1054 and produced the Crab Nebula. Electromagnetic wavelengths contains little energy. Electro-magnetic radiation with short wavelengths contains a great amount of energy. Scientists name the different regions of the electromagnetic spectrum according to their wavelengths. (See figure 1.) Radio waves have the longest wavelengths, ranging from a few centimeters from crest to crest to thousands of kilometers. Micro-waves range from a few centimeters to about 0.1 cm. Infrared radiation falls between 700 nanometers and 0.1 cm. (Nano means one radiation from radio to gamma rays has been detected from this object, and each section of the spectrum tells a different piece of the story.

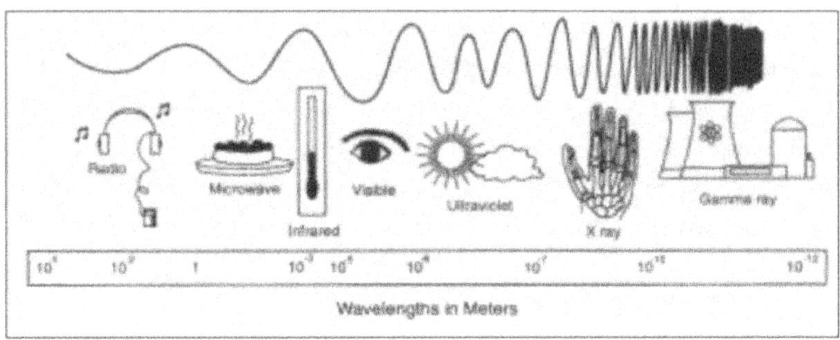

Electromagnetic Spectrum

For most of history, humans used only visible light to explore the skies. With basic tools and the human eye, we developed sophisticated methods of time keeping and calendars. Telescopes were invented in the 17th century. Astronomers then mapped the sky in greater detail—still with visible light. They learned about the temperature, constituents, distribution, and the motions of stars.

In the 20th century, scientists began to explore the other regions of the spectrum. Each region provided new evidence about the universe. Radio waves tell scientists about many things: the distribution of gases in our Milky Way Galaxy, the power in the great jets of material spewing from the centers of some other galaxies, and details about magnetic fields in space. The first radio astronomers unexpectedly found cool hydrogen gas distributed throughout the Milky Way. Hydrogen atoms are the building blocks for all matter. The remnant radiation from the Big Bang, the beginning of the universe, shows up in the microwave spectrum.

Infrared studies (also radio studies) tell us about molecules in space. For example, an infrared search reveals huge clouds of formaldehyde in space, each more than a million times more massive than the Sun. Some ultraviolet light comes from powerful galaxies very far away. Astronomers have yet to understand the highly energetic engines in the centers of these strange objects.

Ultraviolet light studies have mapped the hot gas near our Sun (within about 50 light years). The high energy end of the spectrum—x-rays and gamma rays—provide scientists with information about processes they cannot reproduce here on Earth because they lack the required power. Nuclear physicists use strange stars and galaxies as a laboratory. These objects are pulsars, neutron stars, black holes, and active galaxies. Their study helps scientists better understand the behavior of matter at extremely high densities and temperatures in the presence of intense electric and magnetic fields.

Each region of the electromagnetic spectrum provides a piece of the puzzle. Using more than one region of the electromagnetic spectrum at a time gives scientists a more complete picture. For example, relatively cool objects, such as star-forming clouds of gas and dust, show up best in the radio and infrared spectral region. Hotter objects, such as stars, emit most of their energy at visible and ultraviolet wavelengths. The most energetic objects, such as supernova explosions, radiate intensely in the x-ray and gamma ray regions.

There are two main techniques for analyzing starlight. One is called spectroscopy and the other photometry. Spectroscopy spreads out the different wavelengths of light into a spectrum for study. Photometry measures the quantity of light in specific wavelengths or by combining all

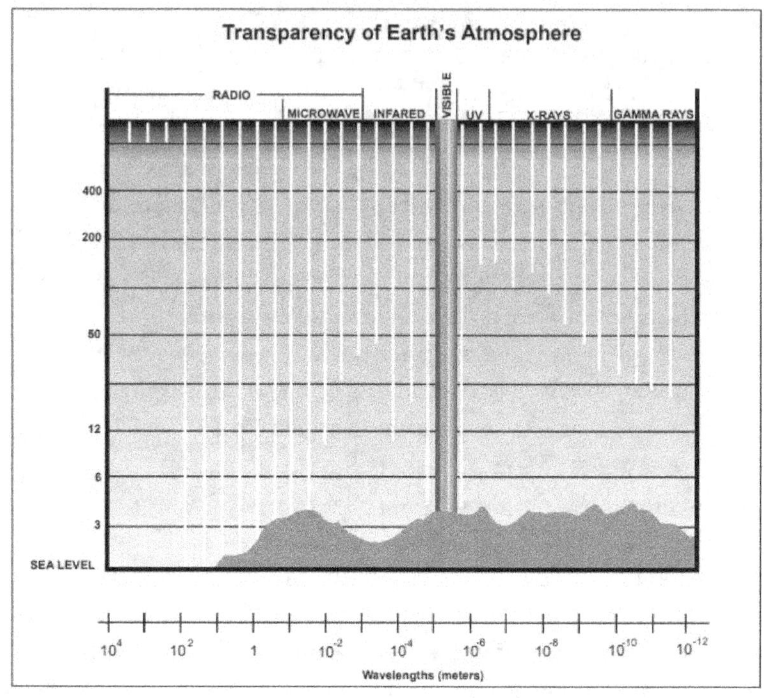

Transparency of Earth's Atmosphere

wavelengths. Astronomers use many filters in their work. Filters help astronomers analyze particular components of the spectrum. For example, a red filter blocks out all visible light wavelengths except those that fall around 600 nanometers (it lets through red light).

Unfortunately for astronomical research, Earth's atmosphere acts as a filter to block most wavelengths in the electromagnetic spectrum. (See Unit 1.) Only small portions of the spectrum actually reach the surface. (See figure 2.) More pieces of the puzzle are gathered by putting observatories at high altitudes (on mountain tops) where the air is thin and dry, and by flying instruments on planes and balloons. By far the best viewing location is outer space.

Unit Goals

• To investigate the visible light spectrum.

• To demonstrate the relationship between energy and wavelength in the electromagnetic spectrum.

Teaching Strategy

Because of the complex apparatus required to study some of the wavelengths of the electromagnetic spectrum and the danger of some of the radiation, only the visible light spectrum will be studied in the activities that follow. Several different methods for displaying the visible spectrum will be presented. Some of the demonstrations will involve sunlight, but a flood or spotlight may be substituted. For best results, these activities should be conducted in a room where there is good control of light.

ACTIVITY:

Simple Spectroscope Description:

A basic hand-held spectroscope is made from a diffraction grating and a paper tube.

Objective:

To construct a simple spectroscope with a diffraction grating and use it to analyze the colors emitted by various light sources.

National Education Standards:

Mathematics

Measurement

Connections

Science Systems, order, & organization

Change, constancy, & measurement

Abilities necessary to do scientific inquiry

Abilities of technological design Technology

Understand engineering design

Materials:

Diffraction grating, 2-cm square (See management and tips section.) Paper tube (tube from toilet paper roll) Poster board square (5 by 10-cm) Masking tape Scissors Razor blade knife 2 single-edge razor blades Spectrum tubes and power supply (See management and tips section.) Pencil

Procedure:

1. Using the pencil, trace around the end of the paper tube on the poster board. Make two circles and cut them out. The circles should be just larger than the tube's opening.

2. Cut a 2-centimeter square hole in the center of one circle. Tape the diffraction grating square over the hole. If students are making their own spectroscopes, it may be better if an adult cuts the squares and the slot in step 4 below.

3. Tape the circle with the grating inward to one end of the tube.

4. Make a slot cutter tool by taping two single-edge razor blades together with a piece of poster board between. Use the tool to make parallel cuts about 2 centimeters long across the middle of the second circle. Use the razor blade knife to cut across the ends of the cuts to form a narrow slot across the middle of the circle.

5. Place the circle with the slot against the other end of the tube. While holding it in place, observe a light source such as a fluorescent tube. Be sure to look through the grating end of the spectroscope. The spectrum will appear off to the side from the slot. Rotate the circle with the slot until the spectrum is as wide as possible. Tape the circle to the end of the tube in this position. The spectroscope is complete.

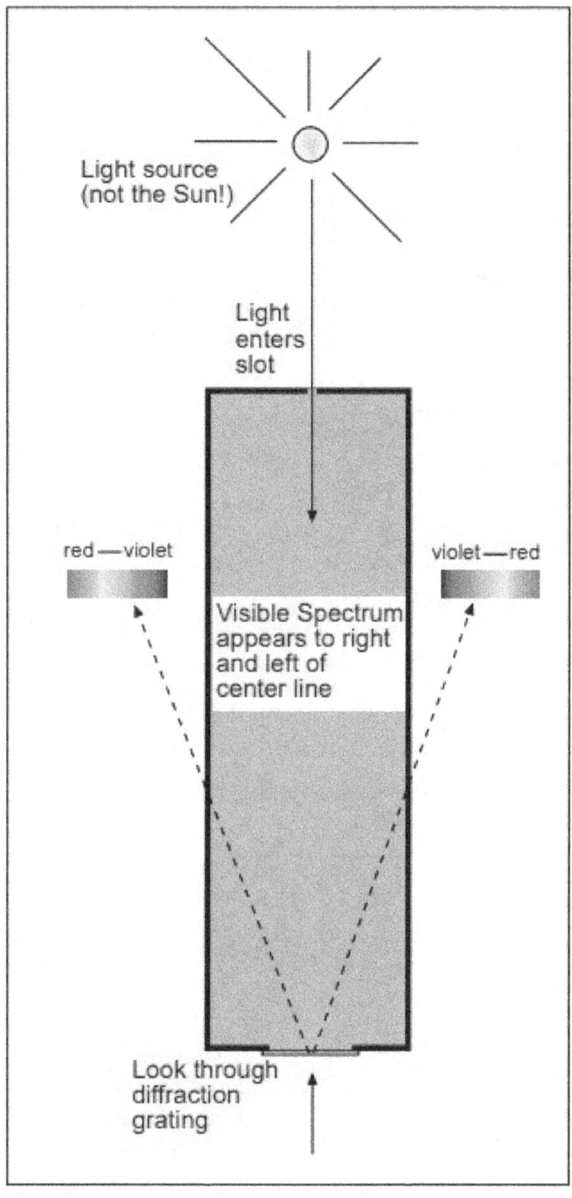

Light source
(not the Sun!)
Light
enters
slot
red—violet
violet—red
Visible Spectrum
appears to right
and left of
center line
Look through
diffraction
grating

6. Examine various light sources with the spectroscope. If possible, examine nighttime street lighting. Use particular caution when examining sunlight. Do not look directly into the Sun.

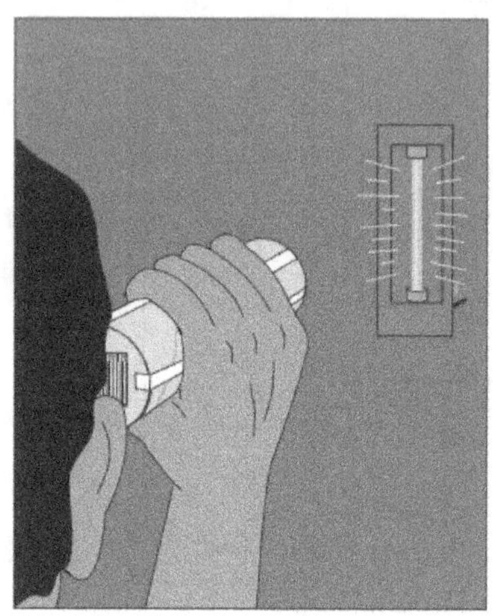 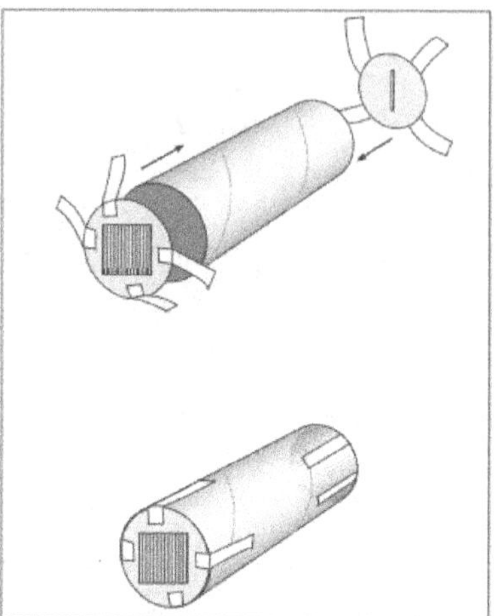

Background:

Simple spectroscopes, like the one described here, are easy to make and offer users a quick look at the color components of visible light. Different light sources (incandescent, fluorescent, etc.) may look the same to the naked eye but will appear differently in the spectroscope. The colors are arranged in the same order but some may be missing and their intensity will vary. The appearance of the spectrum displayed is distinctive and can tell the observer what the light source is.

Management and Tips:

The analytical spectroscope activity that follows adds a measurement scale to the spectroscope design. The scale enables the user to actually measure the colors displayed. As will be described in greater detail in that activity, the specific location of the colors are like fingerprints when it comes to identifying the composition of the light source. Refer to the background and management tips section for the Analytical Spectroscope activity for information on how diffraction gratings produce spectra.

Spectroscopes can be made with glass prisms but prisms are heavy. Diffraction grating spectroscopes can do the same job but are much lighter. A diffraction grating can spread out the spectrum more than a prism can. This ability is called dispersion. Because gratings are smaller and lighter, they are well suited for spacecraft where size and weight are important considerations. Most research telescopes have some kind of grating spectrograph attached. Spectrographs are spectroscopes that provide a record, photographic or digital, of the spectrum observed.

Many school science supply houses sell diffraction grating material in sheets or rolls. One sheet is usually enough for every student in a class to have a piece of grating to build his or her own spectroscope. Holographic diffraction gratings work best for this activity. Refer to the note on the source for holographic grating in the next activity. A variety of light sources can be used for this activity, including fluorescent and incandescent lights and spectra tubes with power supplies. Spectra tubes and the power supplies are available from school science supply catalogs. It may be possible to borrow tubes and supplies from another school if your school does not have them. The advantage of spectrum tubes is that they provide spectra from different gases such as hydrogen and helium. When using the spectroscope to observe sunlight, students should look at reflected sunlight such as light bouncing off clouds or light colored concrete. Other light sources include streetlights (mercury, low-pressure sodium, and high-pressure sodium), neon signs, and candle flames.

X

COLLECTING ELECTROMAGNETIC RADIATION

Except for rock samples brought back from the Moon by Apollo astronauts, cosmic ray particles that reach the atmosphere, and meteorites and comet dust that fall to Earth, the only information about objects in space comes to Earth in the form of electromagnetic radiation. How astronomers collect this radiation determines what they learn from it. The most basic collector is the human eye. The retina at the back of the eye is covered with tiny antennae—called rods and cones—that resonate with incoming light. Resonance with visible electromagnetic radiation stimulates nerve endings, which send messages to the brain that are interpreted as visual images. Cones in the retina are sensitive to the colors of the visible spectrum, while the rods are most sensitive to black and white.

Until the early 1600s, astronomers had only their eyes and a collection of geometric devices to observe the universe and measure locations of stellar objects. They concentrated on the movements of planets and transient objects such as comets and meteors. However, when Galileo Galilei used the newly invented telescope to study the Moon, planets, and the Sun, our knowledge of the universe changed dramatically. He was able to observe moons circling Jupiter, craters on the Moon, phases of Venus, and spots on the Sun. Note: Galileo did his solar observations by projecting light through his telescope on to a white surface—a technique that is very effective even today. Never look directly at the Sun!

Galileo's telescope and all optical telescopes that have been constructed since are collectors of electromagnetic radiation. The objective or front lens of Galileo's telescope was only a few centimeters in diameter. Light rays falling on that lens were bent and concentrated into a narrow beam that emerged through a second lens, entered his eye, and landed on his retina. The lens diameter was much larger than the diameter of the pupil of Galileo's eye, so it collected much more light than Galileo's unaided eye could gather. The telescope's lenses magnified the images of distant objects three times.

Since Galileo's time, many huge telescopes have been constructed. Most have employed big mirrors as the light collector. The bigger the mirror or lens, the more light could be gathered and the fainter the source that the astronomer can detect. The famous 5-meter-diameter Hale Telescope on Mt. Palomar is able to gather 640,000 times the amount of light a typical eye could receive. The amount of light one telescope receives compared to the human eye is its light gathering power (LGP). Much larger even than the Hale Telescope is the Keck Telescope that has an effective diameter of 10 meters. Its light gathering power is two and a half million times that of the typical eye. Although NASA's Hubble Space Telescope, in orbit above Earth's atmosphere, has only a LGP of 144,000, it has the advantage of an unfiltered view of the universe. Furthermore, its sensitivity extends into infrared and ultraviolet wavelengths.

Once a telescope collects photons, the detection method becomes important. Telescopes are collectors, not detectors. Like all other telescopes, the mirror of the Hubble Space Telescope is a photon collector that gathers the photons to a focus so a detector can pick them up. It has several filters that move in front of the detector so images can be made at specific wavelengths.

In the early days, astronomers recorded what they saw through telescopes by drawing pictures and taking notes. When photography was invented, astronomers replaced their eyes with photographic plates. A photographic plate is similar to the film used in a modern camera except that the emulsion was supported on glass plates instead of plastic. The emulsion collected photons to build images and spectra. Astronomers also employed the photo-multiplier tube, an electronic device for counting photons.

The second half of this century saw the development of the Charge Coupled Device (CCD), a computer-run system that collects photons on a small computer chip. CCDs have now replaced the photographic plate for most astronomical observations. If astronomers require spectra, they insert a spectrograph between the telescope and the CCD. This arrangement provides digital spectral data.

Driving each of these advances was the need for greater sensitivity and accuracy of the data. Photographic plates, still used for wide-field studies, collect up to about five percent of the photons that fall on them. A CCD collects 85 to 95 percent of the photons. Because CCDs are small and can only observe a small part of the sky at a time, they are especially suited for deep space observations.

Because the entire electromagnetic spectrum represents a broad range of wavelengths and energies, no one detector can record all types of radiation. Antennas are used to collect radio and microwave energies. To collect very faint signals, astronomers use large parabolic radio antennas that reflect incoming radiation to a focus much in the same way reflector telescopes collect and concentrate light. Radio receivers at the focus convert the radiation into electric currents that can be studied. Sensitive solid state heat detectors measure infrared radiation, higher in energy and shorter in wavelength than radio and microwave radiation. Mirrors in aircraft, balloons, and orbiting spacecraft can concentrate infrared radiation onto the detectors that work like CCDs in the infrared

range. Because infrared radiation is

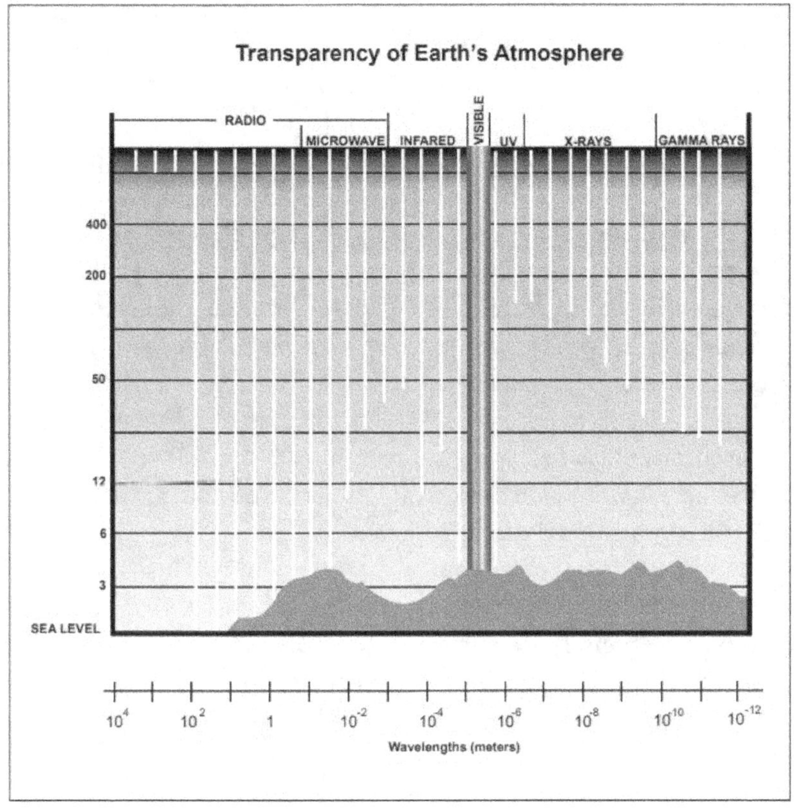

associated with heat, infrared detectors must be kept at very low temperatures lest the telescope's own stored heat energy interferes with the radiation coming from distant objects.

A grazing-incidence instrument consists of a mirrored cone that directs high-energy radiation to detectors placed at the mirror's apex. Different mirror coatings are used to enhance the reflectivity of the mirrors to specific wavelengths.

X-ray spacecraft, such as the Chandra X-ray Observatory, also use grazing-incidence mirrors and solid state detectors while gamma ray spacecraft use a detector of an entirely different kind. The Compton Gamma-Ray Observatory has eight 1-meter-sized crystals of sodium iodide that detect incoming gamma rays as the observatory orbits Earth. Sodium iodide is sensitive to gamma rays but not to optical and radio wavelengths. The big crystal is simply a detector of photons—it does not focus them.

Today, astronomers can choose to collect and count photons, focus the photons to build up an image, or disperse the photons into their various wavelengths. High-energy photons are usually detected with counting techniques. The other wavelengths are detected with counting (photometry), focusing methods (imaging), or dispersion methods (spectroscopy). The particular instrument or combination of instruments astronomers choose depends not only on the spectral region to be observed, but also on the object under observation. Stars are point sources in the sky. Galaxies are not. So the astronomer must select a combination that provides good stellar images or good galaxy images.

Another important property of astronomical instruments is resolution. This is the ability to separate two closely-spaced objects from each other. For example, a pair of automobile headlights appears to be one bright light when seen in the distance along a straight highway. Close up, the headlights resolve into two. Since telescopes, for example, have the effect of increasing the power of our vision, they improve our resolution of distant objects as well. The design and diameter of astronomical instruments determines whether the resolution is high or low. For stellar work, high resolution is important so the astronomer can study one star at a time. For galaxy work, the individual stars in a galaxy may often not be as important as the whole ensemble of stars.

Unit Goals

· To demonstrate how electromagnetic radiation can be collected and detected through the use of mirrors, lenses, and infrared detectors.

· To illustrate how the use of large instruments for collecting electromagnetic radiation increases the quantity and quality of data collected.

Teaching Strategy

Because many of the wavelengths in the electromagnetic spectrum are difficult or dangerous to work with, activities in this section concentrate on the visible spectrum, the near infrared, and radio wavelengths. Several of the activities involve lenses and mirrors. The Visible Light Collector activity provides many tips for obtaining a variety of lenses and mirrors at little or no cost.

ACTIVITY: Visible Light Collectors

(Telescopes)

Description:

A simple refractor telescope is made from a mailing tube, Styrofoam tray, rubber cement, and some lenses and the principle behind a reflector telescope is demonstrated.

Objectives:

To build a simple astronomical telescope from two lenses and some tubes. To use a concave mirror to focus an image.

National Education Standards:

Mathematics

Measurement

Connections

Science

Change, constancy, & measurement Abilities of technological design Understanding about science & technology History of science

Technology

Understand relationships & connections among technologies & other fields Understand cultural, social, economic, & political effects of technology Understand the influence of technology on history Understand, select, & use information & communication technologies

Materials:

Paper mailing tube (telescoping—1 inside tube and 1 outside tube) Styrofoam trays (1 thick and 1 thin) Lenses (1 large and 1 small. See note about lenses.) Metric ruler Razor blade knife Cutting surface Marker pen Rubber cement Fine grade sandpaper Concave makeup mirror Electric holiday candle or other small light Dark room Sheet of white paper Assorted convex lenses (See section on Obtaining and Making Lenses and Mirrors.)

Part 1 - Procedure for Making a Refractor Telescope:

1. Cut a short segment from the end of the outside mailing tube. This circle will be used for tracing only. Place the circle from the larger tube on the thick tray. Using a marker pen, trace the inside of the circle on to the bottom of the tray three times.

2. Lay the large (objective) lens in the center of one of the three large circles. Trace the lens' outline on the circle.

3. Cut the circle with the lens tracing from the tray using the razor blade knife. Be sure to place the Styrofoam on a safe cutting surface. Cut out the lens tracing, but when doing so, cut inside the line so that the hole is slightly smaller than the diameter of the lens.

4. Before cutting out the other two large circles, draw smaller circles inside them approximately equal to 7/8ths of the diameter of the large lens. Cut out both circles inside and out.

5. Coat both sides of the inner circle (the one that holds the lens) with rubber cement and let dry. Coat just one side each of the other two circles with cement and let dry. For a better bond, coat again with glue and let dry.

6. Insert the lens into the inner circle. It will be snug. Press the other circles to either side. Be careful to align the circles properly. Because the outside circles have smaller diameters than the lens, the lens is firmly held in place. You have completed the objective lens mounting assembly

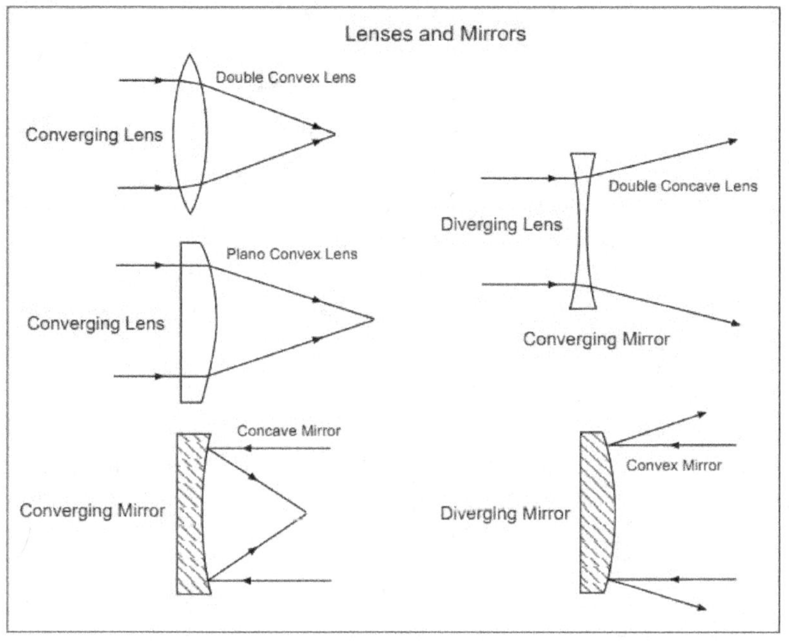

7. Repeat steps 1- 6 for the inside tube and use the smaller lens for tracing. However, because the eyepiece lens is thinner than the objective lens, cut the inner circle from the thin tray.

8. After both lens mounting assemblies are complete, lay the fine sandpaper on a flat surface and gradually sand the edges of each completed lens mounting assembly to make them smooth. Stop sanding when the assemblies are just larger than the inside diameter of the corresponding tube. With a small amount of effort, the assembly will compress slightly and slip inside the tube. (Do not insert them yet.) Friction will hold them in place. If the lens assemblies get too loose, they can be held firmly with glue or tape.

9. Hold the two lens assemblies up and look through the lenses. Adjust their distances apart and the distance to your eye until an image comes into focus. Look at how far the two lenses are from each other. Cut a segment from the outside and the inside tube that

together equal two times the distance you just determined when holding up the lenses. Use the sandpaper to smooth any rough edges on the tubes after cutting.

10. Carefully, so as not to smudge the lenses, insert the large lens assembly into one end of the outside tube and the eyepiece lens assembly into the end of the inside tube. Slip the inside tube into the outside tube so that the lenses are at opposite ends. Look through the eyepiece towards some distant object and slide the small tube in and out of the large tube until the image comes into focus.

11. (Optional) Decorate the outside tube with marker pens or glue a picture to it.

Background:

The completed telescope is known as a refractor. Refractor means that light passing through the objective lens is bent (refracted) before reaching the eyepiece. Passing through the eyepiece, the light is refracted again.

This refraction inverts the image. To have an upright image, an additional correcting lens or prism is placed in the optical path. Astronomers rarely care if images are right-side-up or up-sidedown. A star looks the same regardless of orientation. However, correcting images requires the use of extra optics that diminish the amount of light collected. Astronomers would rather have bright, clear images than right-side-up images. Furthermore, images can be corrected by inverting and reversing photographic negatives or correcting the image in a computer.

Management and Tips:

Refer to the end of this activity for ideas on how to obtain suitable lenses. PVC plumbing pipes can be used for the telescoping tubes. Purchase tube cutoffs of different diameters at a hardware store. Make sure the cutting of the outside circles in the Styrofoam is precise. A circle cut too small will fall through the tube. If students do cut circles too small, the diameter of the circles can be increased by adding one or more layers of masking tape.

Part 2 - Procedure for Demonstrating the Reflector Telescope Principle:

1. Light the electric candle in a darkened room.

2. Bring the concave makeup mirror near the candle flame and tilt and turn it so that reflected light from the lamp focuses on a sheet of white paper.

3. Experiment with different lenses to find one suitable for turning the makeup mirror into a simple reflector telescope. Hold the lens near your eye and move it until the reflected light from the mirror comes into focus.

Background:

Many reflecting telescopes gather light from distant objects with a large concave mirror that directs the light toward a secondary mirror which then focuses the light onto a detector. The concave mirror used in this demonstration shows how a concave mirror can concentrate light to form a recognizable image. The image produced with a makeup mirror will not be well focused because such mirrors are inexpensively produced from molded glass rather than from carefully shaped and polished glass. Furthermore, proper focusing requires that the mirror be precisely shaped in a parabolic curve.

Reflecting telescope mirrors can be made very large and this increases the amount of light they can capture. Refer to the telescope performance activity that follows for information on light gathering power. Small telescopes can only detect bright or nearby stars. Large telescopes (over 4 meters in diameter) can detect objects several billion times fainter than the brightest stars visible to our naked eyes.

Large astronomical telescopes do not employ eyepieces. Rather, light falls on photographic film, photometers, or charged coupled devices (CCDs). This demonstration shows how an image forms on a flat surface. Covering the surface with photographic film will produce a crude picture. Although astronomers have converted to CCDs for most observations, photography is still employed for some applications. Rather than film, astronomers usually prefer photographic emulsions on sheets of glass, which are more stable over time.

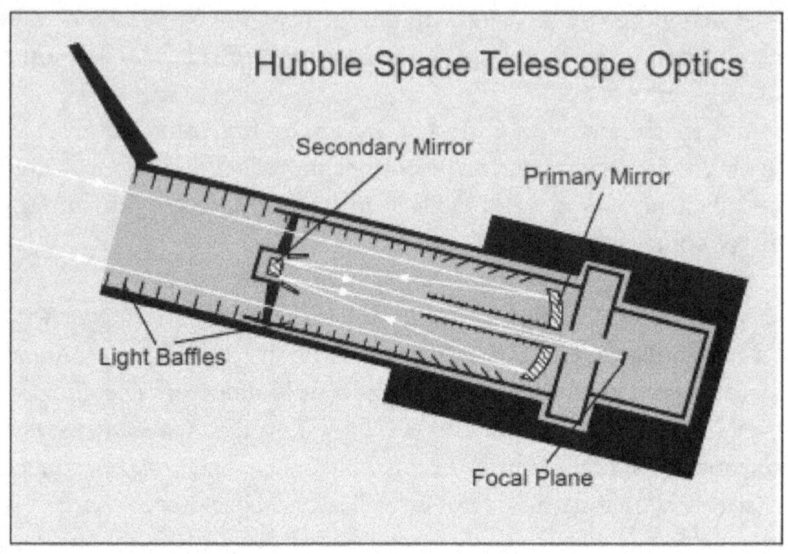

Hubble Space Telescope Optics
Secondary Mirror
Primary Mirror
Light Baffles
Focal Plane

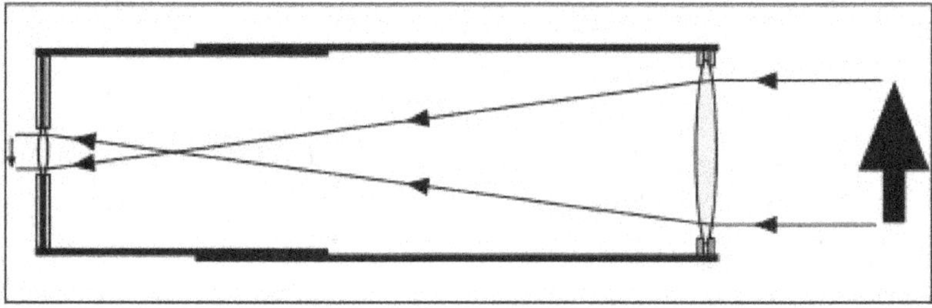

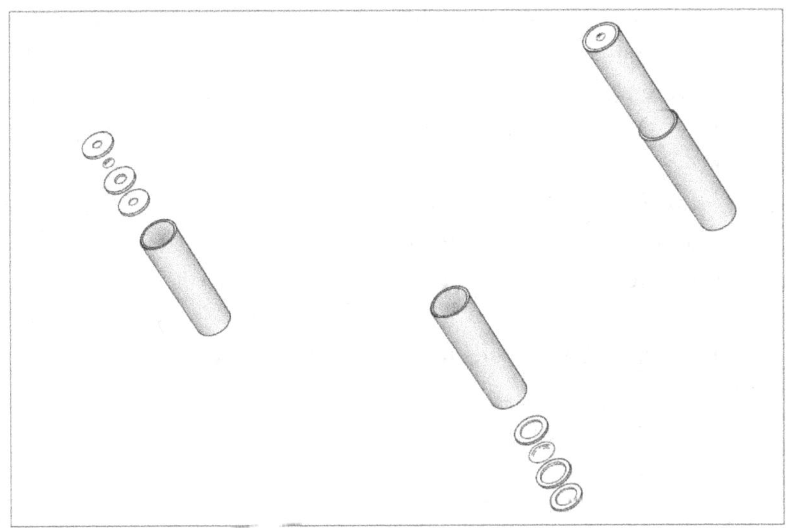

Extensions:

• Bring commercially-made telescopes, spyglasses, and binoculars into the classroom. Compare magnification, resolution, and light gathering power to that of the telescope made here. Learn how these optical instruments function.

• Invite local amateur astronomy clubs to host "star parties" for your students.

• Why are the largest astronomical telescopes made with big objective mirrors rather than big objective lenses?

• Find out how different kinds of reflecting telescopes such as the Newtonian, Cassegrain, and Coude work.

Obtaining and Making Lenses and Mirrors:

An amazing collection of lenses and mirrors can be obtained at little or no cost through creative scrounging. Ask an optometrist or eyewear store if they will save damaged eyeglass lenses for you. Although not of a quality useful for eyewear, these lenses are very suitable for classroom experimentation. Bifocals and trifocals make fascinating magnifying lenses. Fill a spherical glass flask with water to make a lens. Water-filled cylindrical glass or plastic bottles make magnifiers that magnify in one direction only. Aluminized mylar plastic stretched across a wooden frame makes a good front surface plane mirror. A Plexiglas mirror can be bent to make a "funhouse" mirror. Low-reflectivity plane mirrors can be made from a sheet glass backed with black paper. Ask the person in charge of audiovisual equipment at the school to save the lenses from any broken or old projectors that are being discarded. Projector and camera lenses are actually made up of many lenses sandwiched together. Dismantle the lens mounts to obtain several usable lenses. Check rummage sales and flea markets for binoculars and old camera lenses.

ACTIVITY:

Telescope Performance Description:

Students compare and calculate the light gathering power of lenses.

Objective: To determine the ability of various lenses and mirrors to gather light.

National Education Standards:

Mathematics

Patterns, functions, & algebra Geometry & spatial sense Measurement Problem solving Connections

Science

Change, constancy, & measurement Abilities necessary to do scientific inquiry Understandings about science & technology

Technology

Understand characteristics & scope of technology Understand, select, & use information & communication technologies

Materials:

Gray circles on page 00 White paper punchouts from a three-hole paper punch White paper Double convex lenses of different diameters Metric ruler Small telescope from previous activity Binoculars (optional) Overhead projector Transparency copy of master on page 00 Resolving Power chart on page 00 Astronomical telescope (optional)

Procedure – Light Gathering Power:

1. Have students examine several different double convex lenses.
2. Compare the ability of each lens to gather light by focusing the light from overhead fixtures onto a piece of white paper. Which lens produces a brighter image? Be sure to hold the lenses parallel to the paper.
3. Compare the light gathering power of five imaginary lenses (gray circles) by placing small white paper circles (punchouts) on each. The number of punchouts represents the number of photons collected at a moment of time. Students may draw their own circles with compasses for this step.
4. What is the mathematical relationship between the number of punchouts that a circle can hold and the circle's diameter? How did you arrive at this conclusion?

Procedure – Magnification:

1. Make an overhead transparency of the grid. Project the transparency on a screen so that it is as large as possible and position the projector to reduce the "keystone" effect.
2. Roll a paper tube the same diameter as the front end of the telescope or binocular lens you are using. The length of the tube should be the same length as the telescope or binocular. Because binoculars use prisms to reduce their size (see illustration), make the tube two times longer than the distance between the front and rear lenses of the binoculars.
3. Have students stand in the middle or rear of the room. They should stand at a distance that will permit the telescope or binoculars to focus on the screen. Many optical instruments have minimum focal distances.
4. Looking first through the tube, have students count the number of squares they can see at a time from one side of the tube to the other.
5. Using the binoculars (one eye only) or the telescope, have students repeat the counting of squares.
6. The ratio of the number of squares seen in the tube versus the

number seen in the binoculars is a rough approximation of the magnification power of the instrument. For example, if the student can see three squares with the tube and only one with the telescope, the magnification power of the telescope is approximately 3 because a single square spanned the telescope instead of three squares with a tube of a similar diameter and length.

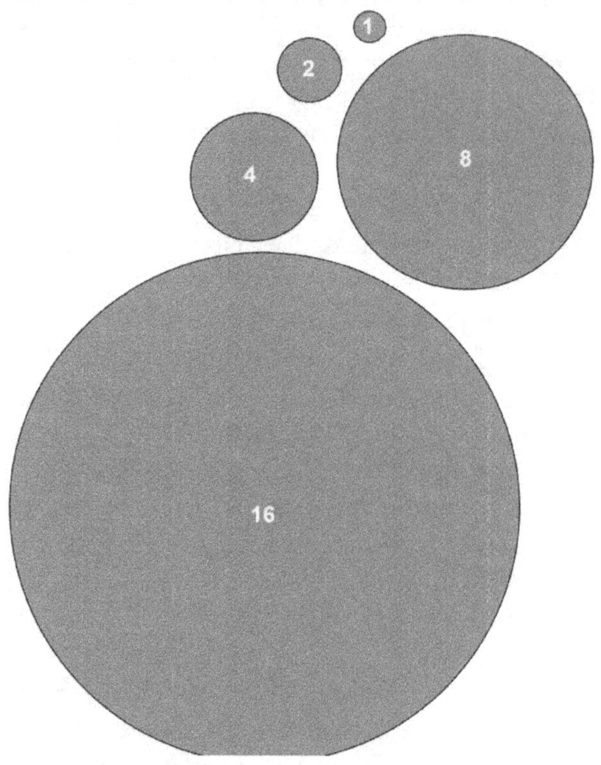

Magnification Grid

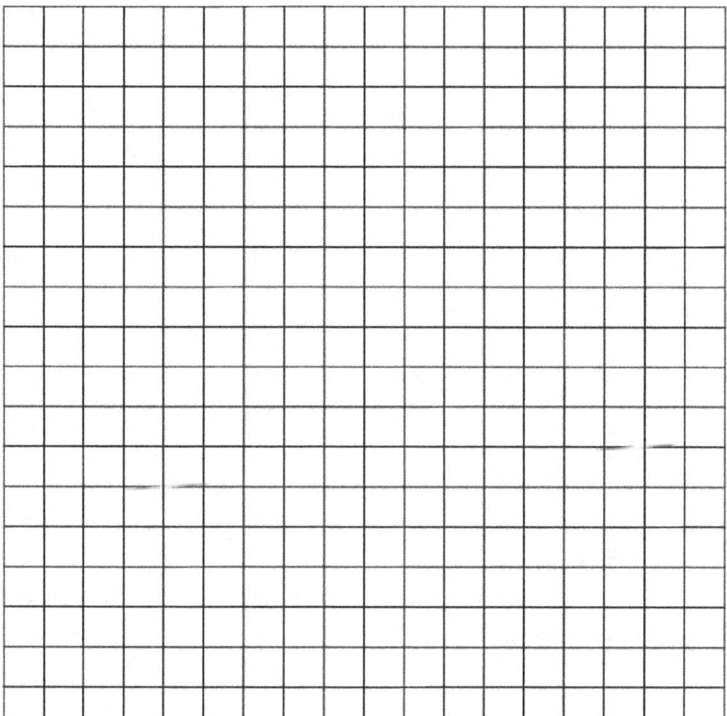

Procedure – Resolving Power:

1. Tape to the front board.

2. Have students stand near the rear of the roomand look at the dots. Ask them to look at the squares and state how many dots they see.

3. Have students repeat the observation with the aid of a telescope or binoculars.

Background:

Light Gathering Power – In a dark room, the pupil of the eye gets bigger to collect more of the dim light. In bright sunlight, the pupil gets smaller so that too much light is not let into the eye. A telescope is a device that effectively makes the pupil as large as the objective lens or mirror.

A telescope with a larger objective lens (front lens) or objective mirror collects and concentrates more light than a telescope with a smaller lens or mirror. Therefore, the larger telescope has a greater light gathering power than the smaller one. The mathematical relationship that expresses light gathering power (LGP) follows:

$$\frac{LGP_A}{LGP_B} = \left(\frac{D_A}{D_B}\right)^2$$

In this equation, A represents the larger telescope and B the smaller telescope or human eye. The diameter of the objective lens or mirror for each telescope is represented by D. Solving this equation yields how much greater the light gathering power (LGP) of the bigger telescope is over the smaller one. For example, if the diameter of the large telescope is 100 cm and the smaller telescope is 10 cm, the light gathering power of the larger telescope will be 100 times greater than that of the smaller scope.

Light gathering power is an important measure of the potential performance of a telescope. If an astronomer is studying faint objects, the telescope

$$\frac{LGP_A}{LGP_B} = \left(\frac{100 \text{ cm}_A}{10 \text{ cm}_B}\right)^2 = \frac{10,000}{100} = 100$$

used must have sufficient light gathering power to collect enough light to make those objects visible. Even with the very largest telescopes, some distant space objects appear so faint that the only way they become visible is through long-exposure photography or by using CCDs. A photographic plate at the focus of a telescope may require several hours of exposure before enough light collects to form an image for an astronomer to study. Unfortunately, very large ground-based telescopes also detect extremely faint atmospheric glow, which interferes with the image. Not having to look through the atmosphere to see faint objects is one of the advantages space-based telescopes have over ground-based instruments.

Magnification – Magnification is often misunderstood as a measure of a telescope's performance. One would think that a telescope with a higher magnification power would perform better than a telescope with a lower power. This is not necessarily so. A telescope with a high magnification power but a low light gathering power will produce highly magnified images that are too faint to see. A rule of thumb in obtaining a telescope is that the magnification of the telescope should be no greater than 25 times the diameter of the large (front) lens in centimeters. For example, a telescope with a front lens with a diameter of 5 centimeters should have a maximum magnification of no more than 125. Anything beyond that will produce a very poor view.

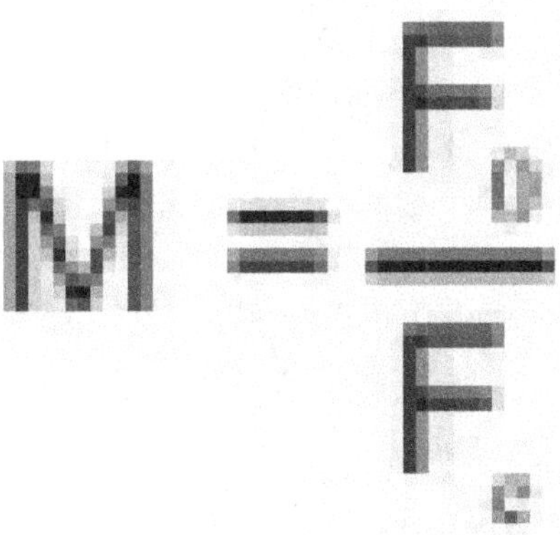

$$M = \frac{F_o}{F_e}$$

The magnification of a telescope is calculated by dividing the focal length of the front lens by the focal length of the eyepiece. The focal length is the distance from the center of the lens to the focal point. With astronomical telescopes, the focal lengths of the various lenses are marked on the housing.

$$\alpha = \frac{11.6}{D}$$

Resolving Power – With telescopes as powerful as the Hubble Space Telescope, resolving power becomes important. Resolving power is the ability of a telescope to separate two closely spaced objects. For example, a bright star to the naked eye might actually be two closely-spaced stars in a telescope. Resolving power is measured in arc seconds. An arc second is 1:3,600[th] of a degree.

Management and Tips:

In this light gathering power activity, younger students can use larger objects such as pennies, washers, or poker chips in place of the paper punchouts. Discs can be eliminated entirely by drawing the circles directly on graph paper and counting the squares to estimate light gathering power of different sized lenses and mirrors. When students notice that the punchouts do not entirely cover the circles, ask them what they should do to compensate for the leftover space. For the activity on magnification and resolving power, use the small telescope constructed in the previous activity. Because of their minimum focal distance, astronomical telescopes will not work for this activity. A toy spyglass and spotter scopes should work.

Assessment:

Collect student sheets and compare answers.

Student Work Sheet Answers:

1A. The ratio of the amount of light a telescope can gather compared to the human eye.

1B. The ability of a telescope to make distant objects appear larger.

1C. The ability of a telescope to distinguish between two closely spaced objects.

2. 100

3. 100

4. 0.058 arc seconds

Extensions:

• Compare the light gathering power of the various lenses you collected with the human eye. Have students measure the diameters, in centimeters, of each lens. Hold a small plastic ruler in front of each student's eye in the class and derive an average pupil diameter for all students. Be careful not to touch eyes with the ruler. If you have an astronomical telescope, determine its light gathering power over the unaided human eye.

• If an astronomical telescope is available, have students calculate the actual magnification power of the telescope with its various lenses.

• Have students calculate the focal length of the lenses used in the light gathering power portion of this activity. The students should focus light from overhead fixtures on the desk top and measure how far above the desk the lens is. This is the focal length.

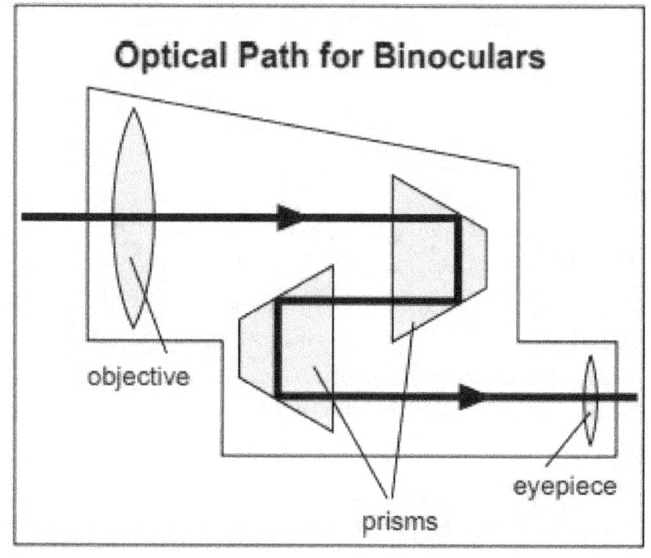

Optical Path for Binoculars
objective
prisms
eyepiece

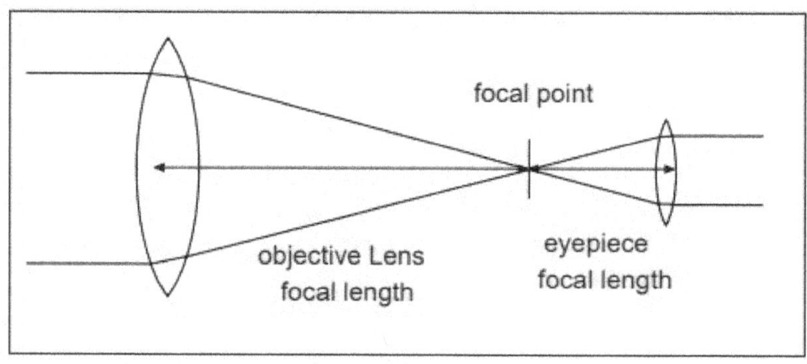

focal point
objective Lens
focal length
eyepiece
focal length

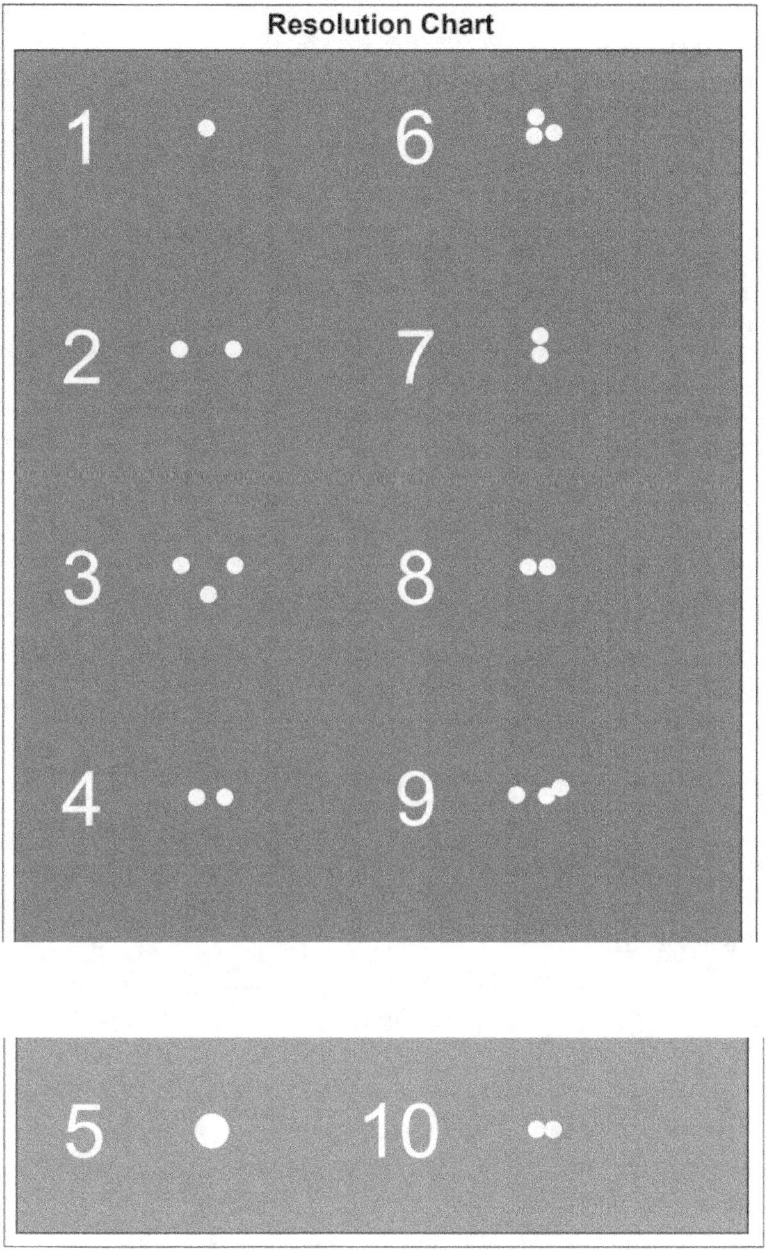
Resolution Chart
1
6
2
7
3
8
4
9
5
10

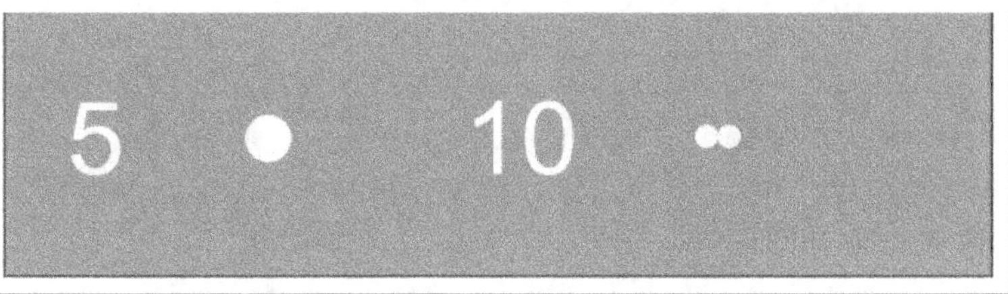

ACTIVITY:
Liquid Crystal IR Detector Description:
Students simulate the detection of infrared radiation using a liquid crystal sheet.
Objective:
To experiment with one method of detecting infrared radiation.
National Education Standards:
Science
Evidence, models, & explanation Properties & changes of properties in matter Transfer of energy Understandings about science & technology
Technology
Understand relationships & connections among technologies & other fields Understand, select, & use information & communication technologies
Materials:
Liquid crystal sheet (available at museums, nature stores, and science supply catalogs)
Table top Procedure:
1. Have a student touch his or her fingertips on a tabletop for 30 seconds. Make sure the student has warm hands.
2. While handling the liquid crystal sheet only by its edges, place it where the fingertips touched the table. Observe what happens over the next several seconds.
Background:
Infrared telescopes have a detector sensitive to infrared light. The telescope is placed as high up in the atmosphere as possible on a mountaintop, in an aircraft or balloon, or flown in space because water vapor in the atmosphere absorbs some of the infrared radiation from space. The human eye is not sensitive to infrared light, but our bodies are. We sense infrared radiation as heat. Because of this association with heat, telescopes and infrared detectors must be kept as cool as possible. Any heat from the

surroundings will create lots of extra infrared signals that interfere with the real signal from space. Astronomers use cryogens such as liquid nitrogen, liquid helium, or dry ice to cool infrared instruments.

This activity uses a liquid crystal detector that senses heat. Also known as cholesteric liquid crystals, the liquid inside the sheet exhibits dramatic changes in colors when exposed to slight differences in temperature within the range of 25 to 32 degrees Celsius. The sheet detects the heat associated with infrared rays.

In the case of an infrared telescope in space, the energy is detected directly by instruments sensitive to infrared radiation. Usually, the data is recorded on computers and transmitted to Earth as a radio signal. Ground-based computers reassemble the image of the objects that created the radiation.

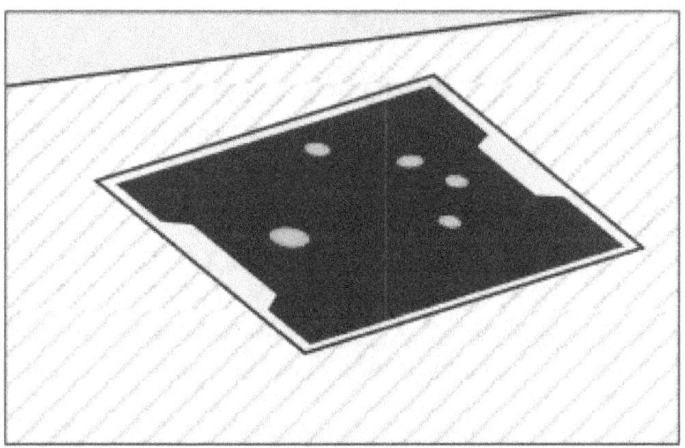

Management and Tips:

Liquid crystal sheets come in many forms. The best sheets for this activity are large enough to fit an entire hand. These sheets also come as postcards and as thermometers. You may be able to find a forehead thermometer made of a strip of liquid crystals.

Do not allow the sheet to come into direct contact with very hot materials as they may damage the sheet. It is important that the student has hands warm enough to leave a heat signature on the tabletop. Also, it is important that the tabletop be relatively cool to start with. If the table is already warm, the image of the fingertips will be masked by the tabletop's heat. This is similar to the situation that would occur inside a spacecraft that is not cooled. Stray infrared signals from the spacecraft would cloud the infrared image from distance objects.

Assessment:

Ask your students why it is important to keep infrared telescopes very cool for accurate observations.

Extensions:

· How was infrared radiation discovered?

· Why do infrared detectors have to be kept cold?

· Learn about cholesteric liquid crystals. An Austrian botanist Freidrich Reinitfer discovered them in 1888.

· Obtain an infrared thermometer for measuring temperatures from a distance. Such thermometers are available from science supply companies. Use the thermometer to measure the temperature of various objects such as a candle flame, beaker of warm water, or ground surfaces in and out of the sunlight.

· Invite a thermal scanning company to demonstrate their equipment to your students. These companies use infrared scanners to form infrared images of homes to isolate areas of heat loss.

XI

DOWN TO EARTH

Although astronomers who work with ground-based telescopes have to deal with bad weather and atmospheric filtering, they do have one advantage over astronomers working with instruments in space. The ground-based astronomers can work directly with their instruments. That means that they can constantly check and adjust their instruments first-hand. Astronomers working with satellite-based instruments must do everything remotely. With the exception of telescopes mounted in the Space Shuttle's payload bay, astronomers can only interact with their instruments via radio transmissions. That means that the instruments have to be mounted on a satellite that provides radio receivers and transmitters, electric power, pointing control, data storage, and a variety of computer-run subsystems.

Data collection, transmission, and analysis are of primary importance to astronomers. The development of photomultiplier tubes and charged coupled devices (CCDs) provides astronomers with an efficient means of collecting data in a digital form, transmitting it via radio, and analyzing it by computer processing. CCDs, for example, convert photons falling on their light sensitive elements into electric signals that are assigned numeric values representing their strength. Spacecraft subsystems convert numeric values into a data stream of binary numbers that are transmitted to Earth. Once received, computers reconvert the data stream to the original numbers that can be processed into images or spectra.

If the satellite is geostationary, these data may be transmitted continuously to ground receiving stations consisting of one or more radio antennas and support equipment. Geostationary satellites orbit in an easterly direction over Earth's equator at an elevation of approximately 40,000 kilometers. They orbit Earth in one day, the same time it takes Earth to rotate, so the satellite remains over the same location on Earth at all times.

Satellites at other altitudes and orbital paths do not stay above one point on Earth. As a result, they remain visible to a particular ground station for a short time and then move out of range. This requires many widely spaced ground stations to collect the satellite's data. In spite of this, the satellite still spends much of its time over parts of Earth where no stations exist (oceans, polar regions, etc.). For this reason, one of the subsystems on astronomical satellites are tape recorders that store data until they can transmit it to ground stations.

In the mid-1980's, NASA began deploying the Tracking and Data Relay Satellite System (TDRSS) into geostationary orbit. The purpose of this system is to relay data to ground stations. Because of their high orbits and their widely spaced station points over Earth's equator, the TDRSS satellites serve as relay points for lower satellites and the Space Shuttle. The system provides nearly continuous contact with spacecraft as they orbit Earth. TDRSS satellites relay data to a receiver at White Sands, New Mexico. From there, the data travel via telephone lines, fiber optic cable, or commercial communications satellites to its destination. Most astrophysics data travels from White Sands to the NASA Goddard Space Flight Center in Maryland for distribution to scientists.

Unit Goal

· To demonstrate how astronomical satellites use technology to collect optical data, transmit that data to Earth, and reassemble it into images.

Approach

The activities in this unit demonstrate the imaging process of astronomical satellites such as the Hubble Space Telescope. Use the Magic Wand and Persistence of Vision activities together or as alternates. The Magic Wand activity shows how images can be divided and reassembled. The Color activity shows how astronomy satellites collect color data and how that data can be reassembled on the ground. The Binary Number and Paint by the Numbers activities familiarize students with the process of data transmission to Earth and its re-assembly into images.

ACTIVITY:

Magic Wand Description:

A recognizable image from a slide projector appears while a white rod moves rapidly across the projector's beam.

Objective:

To demonstrate how an image falling on a CCD array is divided into individual pieces.

National Education Standards:

Science

Evidence, models, & explanation Motions & forces Understandings about science & technology

Technology

Understand relationships & connections among technologies & other fields Understand, select, & use information & communication technologies

Materials:

Slide projector

Color slide of clearly defined object such as Saturn, a building, etc.

1/2-inch dowel, 3 feet long Sheet of white paper

White paint (flat finish) Dark room

Procedure:

1. Paint the dowel white and permit it to dry. (A piece of 3/4-inch PVC water pipe from a hardware store can substitute for the dowel and white paint, and so can a painted meter stick.)

2. Set up the slide projector in the back of the classroom and focus the image of the slide at a distance of about 4 meters away from the projector. Hold the sheet of paper in the beam at the proper distance for easy focusing. Be sure the focus point you select is in the middle of the room and not near a wall.

3. Arrange the students between the focus point and the projector. Darken the room. Hold the dowel in one hand and slowly move it up and down through the projector beam at the focal point. Ask the students to try to identify the image that appears on the dowel.

4. Gradually, increase the speed of the dowel's movement.

5. When the dowel moves very fast, the image becomes clear.

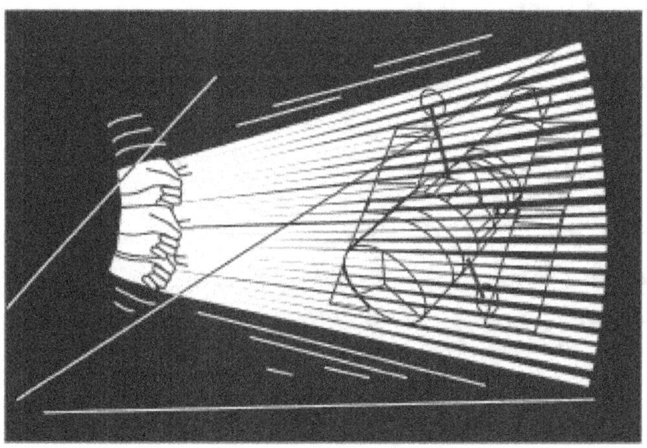

Background:

Because astronomy spacecraft operate in space for many years, the data they collect cannot be recorded on camera film. There is simply no easy way to deliver the film to Earth for processing and to resupply the spacecraft with fresh film. Rather, the satellite instruments collect light from objects and divide it into discrete bits of information and radio them to Earth as a series of binary numbers. This activity demonstrates how images can be divided into many parts and then reassembled into a recognizable picture. By slowly moving the dowel across the slide projector's beam, small fragments of the image are captured and reflected ("radioed") towards the students. Because more and more fragments are sent as the dowel is moved, the image quickly becomes confused in the student's minds. However, as the rod is moved more rapidly, an important property of the eye and brain connection comes into play; light images are momentarily retained. This property is called persistence of vision. As the dowel's movement increases, single lines of the image remain just long enough to combine with the others to form a recognizable image. In this manner, the rapidly moving rod simulates the CCD and the eye/brain interaction simulates the final imaging computer that receives the radioed data and reassembles it for use.

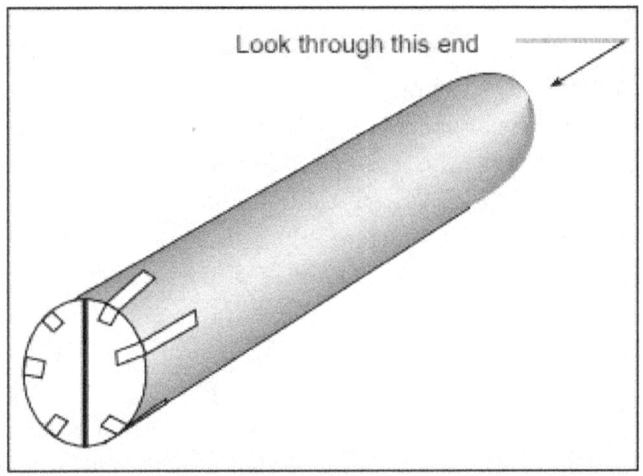

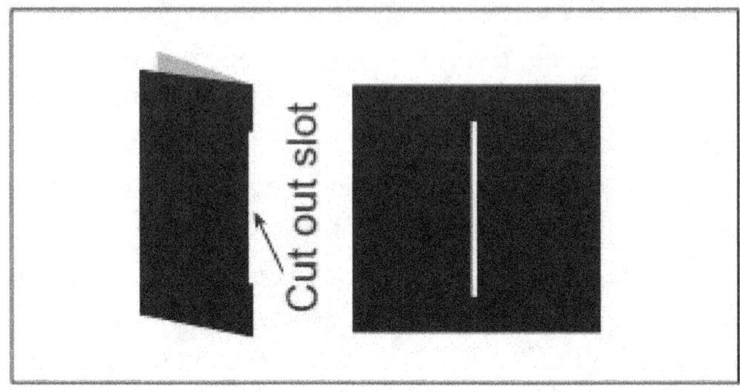

Management and Tips:

By setting up the projector so that its projected image is focused in the middle of the room, the light from the image that falls on the far wall will be out of focus. This will make it more difficult for students to recognize the image until the dowel is passed through the light beam. Be sure to point out that the rod sends ("radios") a fragment of the entire image. When the rod is moved, another image fragment is received. Challenge your students to memorize each fragment as they receive it. The fragments will be quickly forgotten as new fragments are added. It is only when the rod is moved very fast that they will be able to recognize the image. However, if the fragments were received by a computer in a digital form, each fragment would be recorded and an image would be built up at any speed. Relate this activity to the Paint by the Numbers activity on pages 00-00.

Assessment:

Ask students to explain the imaging process as it is demonstrated here and use examples of images in other applications where the images consist of small parts that combine to make a whole.

Extensions:

• How do television studios create and transmit pictures to home receivers?

• How does a CCD work?

• Project some slides. Magnify them as much as possible on a projection screen to see how the complete image consists of many discrete parts.

• Construct a persistence of vision tube. Close off the end of a cardboard tube except for a narrow slit. While looking through the open end of the tube, wave the tube back and forth. A recognizable image will form at the other end of the tube. Use the tube to examine fluorescent lights. Why do slightly darker bands appear across the lights? Hint: Fluorescent lights do not remain on continuously. The light turns on and off with the cycling of AC current. Will using the tube to view an incandescent light have the same effect? Use the tube to examine the picture on a television screen. Why is the TV picture reduced to lines? Hint: Television pictures consist of scan lines.

• A simpler version of the persistence of vision tube can be made with a 10 by 10-centimeter square of black construction paper. Fold the paper in half. Using scissors, cut a narrow slit from the middle of the fold. Open the square up and quickly pass the slit across one eye while looking at some distant objects.

ACTIVITY:

Colors Description:

Students identify the actual colors of objects bathed in monochromatic light and learn how three colors of light can be combined to produce colors ranging from black to white.

Objectives:

• To identify the actual colors of objects bathed in monochromatic light.

• To demonstrate how three colored lights can be combined to produce a wide range of secondary colors.

• To show how space observatories make use of monochromatic filters to collect data on the color of objects in space.

National Education Standards:

Science

Evidence, models, & explanation

Change, constancy, & measurement

Abilities necessary to do scientific inquiry

Properties & changes of properties in matter

Transfer of energy Understandings about science & technology

Technology

Understand relationships & connections
among technologies & other fields

Understand troubleshooting, R & D, invention, innovation, & experimentation

Understand, select, & use information & communication technologies

Materials:

Indoor/outdoor floodlights (red, green, and blue) Adjustable fixtures to hold the lights Projection screen Various colored objects (apple, banana, grapes, print fabrics, etc.) Dark room

Procedure Part 1 - Color Recognition:

1. Prior to class, set up the three floodlights in a row at a distance of about 4 meters from the projection screen so that they each point to the center of the screen. The lights should be spaced about 1 meter apart. When properly aimed, the three lights should blend to produce a nearly white light falling on the screen. Move one or more lights closer to or farther away from the screen to achieve a proper balance.

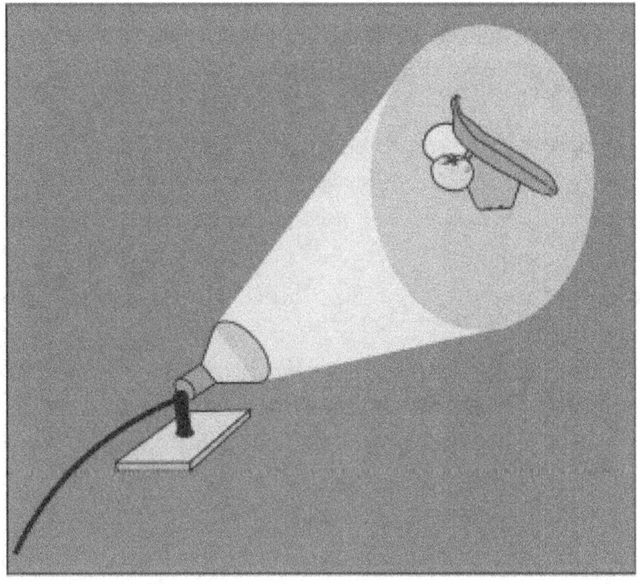

2. Darken the classroom and turn on the red lamp.

3. Hold up the colored objects one at a time. Ask students to make notes on the Color Table as to how bright or dark the objects appear in the red light.

4. Turn off the red light and turn on the green light and repeat with the same objects. Repeat again, but this time use the blue light.

5. Turn on the room lights and show the students the actual colors of the objects.

6. Challenge the students to identify the colors of new objects. Show them the unknown objects in the red, green, and then blue lights. By using their notes, the students should be able to determine the actual colors of the objects.

7. Hold up a Granny Smith or Golden Delicious apple to see if the students can correctly judge its actual color or will instead jump to an erroneous conclusion based on shape.

Procedure Part 2 - Color Shadows:

1. Using the same light and screen setup, darken the room and turn all the floodlights on, hold up your hand between the lights and the screen. Three colored shadows appear—yellow, cyan, and magenta.

2. Move your hand closer to the screen. The shadows will overlap and produce additional colors—red, blue, and green. When all the shadows overlap, there is no color (light) left and the shadow on the screen becomes black.

3. Invite your students to try their "hand" at making shadows.

Background:

Astronomical spacecraft, working in the visible region of the electromagnetic spectrum, collect images of stars and galaxies in various colors. Color filters rotate into the light path so that the detector sees one color at a time. The image in each of these colors is transmitted to Earth as a series of binary numbers. Image processing computers on Earth take each of the images, color them, and combine all the images to reconstruct a multi-colored image representing the true colors of the object. To enhance details in the images, astronomers will use artificial colors or boost the color in one or more wavelengths.

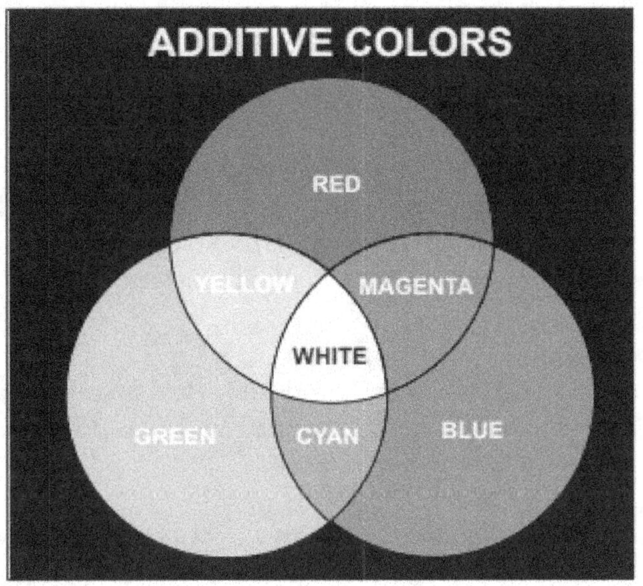

Part 1 of this activity demonstrates the data collection part of the color imaging process. By examining various objects in red, green, and then blue light, the students note that the brightness varies with the illuminating. Using colored lights is equivalent to observing the objects through colored filters. The way each object appears relates to its "real" colors as seen in normal light. By noting subtle differences in brightness in each of the three colored lights, the actual colors of the objects can be identified.

Part 2 of this activity demonstrates how a few basic colors can produce a wide range of colors and hues. When the three lamps are set up properly, the screen appears whitish. When all shadows overlap, they become black; black is the absence of light. In between white and black are red, green, blue, cyan, yellow, and magenta. By moving the floodlights forward and back, a wide range of hues appears.

Management and Tips:

It is difficult to get a pure white screen with indoor/outdoor floodlights. The colors produced by them are not entirely monochromatic. Using much more expensive lamps produces a better white but the whiteness is not significantly enhanced. An alternative to the colored lamps is to obtain red, green, and blue theatrical gels (filters) and place them (one each) on the stage of three overhead projectors. Aiming each of the three projectors to the same place on the screen produces the same effect as the lamps, but the colors are more uniform across the screen and the white is purer.

Assessment:

Collect the color tables of the students. Hold up colored objects in different monochromatic lights and have the students try to identify their white light colors.

Extensions:

• Look at color magazine pictures. How many colors do you see? Examine the pictures with a magnifying glass. How many colors do you see? Also examine the picture on a color television screen.

• What common devices use red, green, and blue to produce colored pictures?

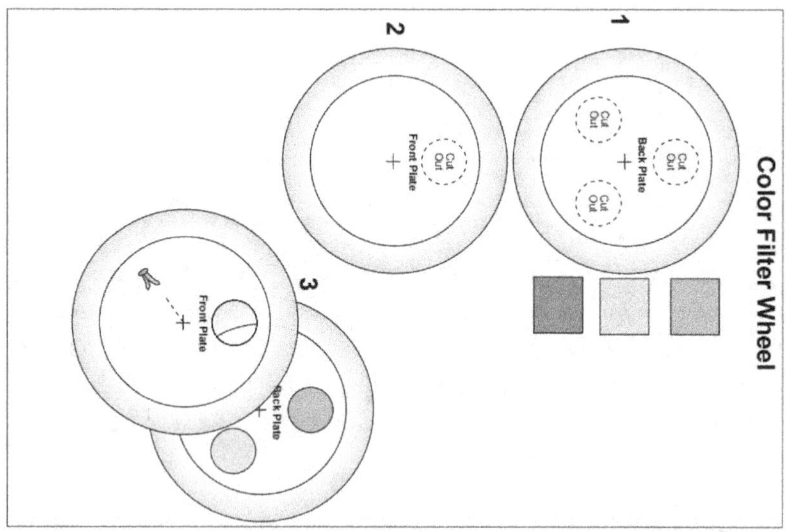

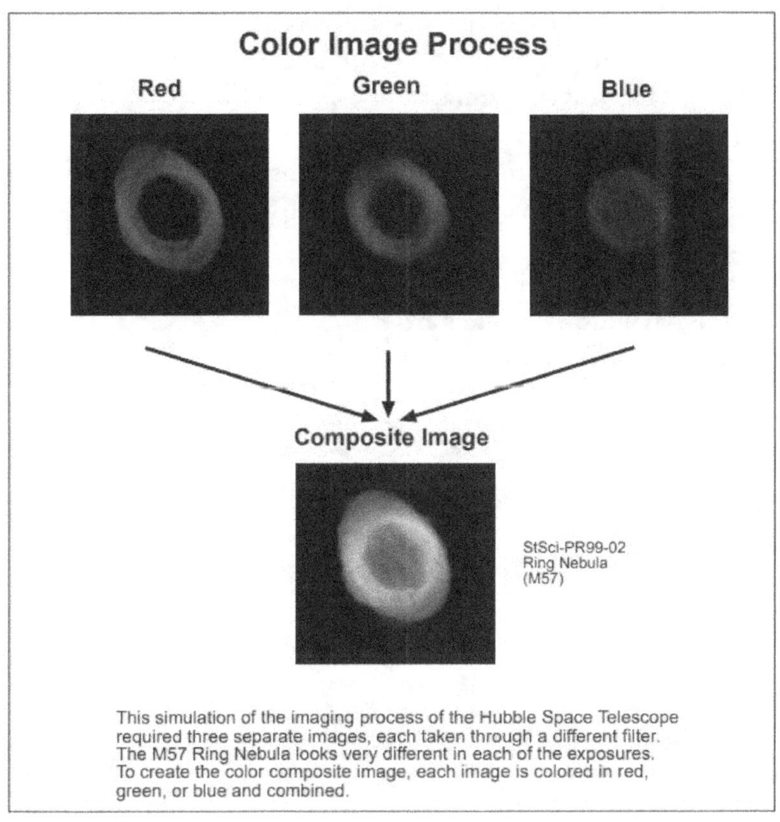

• Is there any difference in the results of mixing colored lights and colored paints?

• Punch a 2-centimeter hole in an opaque piece of paper. Adjusting the distance of the paper to the screen may help students investigate the color additive process.

• This activity also works using colored acetate filters taped over small windows cut into file cards. Sheets of red, green, and blue acetate can be purchased at art supply stores. Students can make their own filter cards and take them home to look through the windows at a variety of objects. Better quality filters, that transmit "purer" colors, can be obtained from theatrical supply stores at a cost comparable to acetate filters. If your school has a theater department, you may be able to obtain filters (gels) from them.

ACTIVITY: Binary Numbers

Description:

Two flashlights are used to demonstrate how astronomy spacecraft transmit images and other scientific data to Earth.

Objective:

To use the binary number system to transmit messages.

National Education Standards:

Mathematics

Number & operation

Patterns, function, & algebra

Measurement

Data analysis, statistics, & probability

Communication

Connections

Representations

Science

Evidence, models, & explanation

Change, constancy, & measurement

Understandings about science & technology

Technology

Understand relationships & connections

among technologies & other fields

Understand cultural, social, economic, & political effects of technology

Understand, select, & use:

Medical technologies

Agricultural technologies & biotechnologies

Energy & power technologies

Information & communication technologies

Transportation technologies

Manufacturing technologies

Construction technologies

Materials:

Two flashlights with pushbutton switches Binary code and data sheets

Procedure:

1. Explain how astronomical spacecraft use the binary system to transmit, via radio waves, images and other scientific data from spacecraft to Earth. Refer to the background section for details on how the system works.

2. Distribute the data sheet and substitution code page to every student. Tap out a six number sequence of the push buttons on the two flashlights. Your right hand flashlight will represent a 1 and your left hand flashlight will represent a 0. As the lights flash, each student should check off the appropriate box in the practice column. To make sense later, the students must check off the boxes representing right or left flashes in the exact sequence of the flashing lights. Refer to the sample on the next page to see how to make the checks.

3. For the practice columns, total up the numbers each sequential flash represents. For example, if all flashes are with the left flashlight, the value is 0+0+0+0+0+0 = 0. If six flashes are all with the right flashlight, the value of the binary number is 63. The first right flash represents a 1, the second is 2, the third is 4, the fourth is 8, the fifth is 16, and the sixth is 32 (1+2+4+8+16+32=63). The following sequence of flashes is 37: Right, Left, Right, Left, Left, Right. After the boxes are filled in, the students total the numbers in the two columns. The answer will give students the total value of the number that was transmitted. (In this activity, the number will represent a letter in a message. With the Hubble Space Telescope, the number will represent the brightness of a particular point on an image.)

4. After the students become familiar with the method, transmit a message to the them. Create the message by referring to the substitution code in the following pages. Replace each word in your message with the corresponding code number. For example, "Hello!" would convert to 7, 4, 11, 11, 24, 38. Next, convert each code number into a binary number. Seven, for example, becomes Right, Right, Right, Left, Left, Left and 24 becomes Left, Left, Left, Right, Right, Left. As you will note in the substitution code, only the first 40 of the 64 possible numbers are used. The remaining numbers can be assigned to common words of your choosing such as "the" and "but," and to short sentences such as "How are you?" Transmit the message by flashing the lights in the proper sequence. Every six flashes represents a binary number that can be converted into a letter or word through the code. Students receive the message by checking the flashes on the data sheet, determining the binary numbers they represent, and then changing the numbers into letters or words.

Background:

Because astronomical spacecraft operate in orbit around Earth, the images they collect of objects in space have to be transmitted to the ground by radio signals. To make this possible, the light from these objects is concentrated on a light sensitive charged coupled device (CCD). The Hubble Space Telescope uses four CCDs arranged in a square. The surface of each CCD is a grid consisting of 800 vertical and 800 horizontal lines that create a total of 640,000 light sensitive squares called pixels for picture elements. With four CCDs, the total number of pixels in the Hubble Space Telescope CCD array is 2,560,000.

Photons of light fall on the CCD array and are converted into digital computer data. A numerical value is assigned to the number of photons received on each of the more than two million pixels. This number represents the brightness of the light falling on each pixel. The numbers range from 0 to 255. This range yields 256 shades of gray ranging from black (0) to white (255).

These numbers are translated into a binary computer code on board the spacecraft. A binary number is a simple numeric code consisting of a specific sequence of on and off radio signals. They are the same codes that are used in computers. A binary number radio transmission can be compared to a flashing light. When the light is on, the value of the signal is a specific number. When the light is off, the value is 0. (In this activity the right flashlight is the 1 and the left flashlight is the 0. Although the activity could be done with 1 flashlight, it would be difficult for students to determine how may 0's are being transmitted when the light is off. Computers precisely time the interval to determine how many 0's are in the sequence. Using a second flashlight for 0's makes it easy for students to determine the number of 0's.)

A binary number usually consists of 8 bits (1 byte). The first bit in the sequence represents a 1. The second bit represents a 2. The remaining 6 bits represent 4, 8, 16, 32, 64, and 128 respectively. If all bits are "on" the value of the binary number is the sum of each bit value—255. If all bits are "off," the value is 0. A sequence of on, off, on, on, off, off, on, and off represents the numbers 1+0+4+8+0+64+0, or 77. To save classroom time, the binary system has been simplified in this activity by using a 6-bit binary code. The total value of a 6-bit code is 64, or 1+2+4+8+16+32.

After the image of the space object is encoded, the binary bits are transmitted by radio waves to a receiving station on the ground. The photons of light that fall on each of the 2,560,000 pixels are now represented by a data set consisting of 20,480,000 binary bits. The computer will convert them to a black and white image of the space object. If a colored image is desired, at least two more images are collected, each one taken through a different colored filter. The data from the three images are combined by a computer into a composite image that shows the actual colors of the object being observed.

Because images collected by the HST and other astronomy spacecraft are digital, astronomers can use computers to manipulate images. This manipulation is roughly analogous to the manipulation of color, brightness, and contrast controls on a television set. The manipulation process is called enhancement and it provides astronomers with a powerful tool for analyzing the light from space objects. To learn more about the imaging process, refer to the following activities in this guide: Paint by the Numbers and Colors.

Management and Tips:

Students may be confused by right and left flashlights when you face them. The right (1) and left (0) flashlights refer to the student's right and left. Look at the columns of marks for each letter you transmit. If the mark is in the right-hand box and represents an on (1) signal, flash the right flashlight. Students will read this as a 0. If the mark is in the left-hand box and represents an off (0) signal, flash your left flashlight. Students will read this as a 1.

Students will sometimes lose track of the light sequence by concentrating on their paper. If you can dim the room lights a bit, which flashlight beam is turned on is easier to see out of the corner of the eye. Also, you can use the light fixtures used in the color activity for the code. Use the green lamp on for a 1 and the red lamp on for a 0.

Students may also become confused by using one number to represent another number. Make sure they understand the sequence of 1's and 0's is the code. The on-off (1-0) code is what is used in the process. However, other things could be used for the 1-0 such as the words "on-off" or even words like "pickle-pineapple." It is the sequence of the words or numbers used that is important. If you have visually impaired students, you can substitute tapping two different surfaces to make two different sounds for them to listen to and interpret as 1's or 0's.

If you wish to use materials other than flashlights for transmitting data, you can make two cards with a large 1 on one card and a 0 on the other. Raise and lower the cards in sequence to represent a binary number.

Assessment:

Check the student sheets to see if they have correctly received the message.

Extensions:

• Have students code binary numbers with a binary coder consisting of several paper desert plates or shallow cups and markers such as jelly beans or breakfast cereal pieces. Arrange the plates in a row and number the first one "1". Mark the plate to the left "2" and the plate to the left of that one "4", etc. Place a small group of markers in the 1 plate. To code the markers into binary numbers, follow these rules: If a plate has two or more markers, remove two markers. Place one of the markers in a discard pile and place the other one in the plate immediately to the left. Continue removing markers from the 1 plate until there is only 1 or 0 left. If plate 2 has 2 or more markers, remove two. Discard one and place the other one in the plate to the left. Continue until all plates have only 1 or 0 markers in them. Starting on the left, write the binary number. Put down a 0 for a plate with no markers in it and a 1 for a plate with a marker in it. To check your work, add up the numbers on all the plates with markers. It should be the same as the number of markers you started with.

• Transmit binary numbers by having four students stand in a row in front of the class. Give each student a card with a 1 on one side and a 0 on the other. Quietly tell the students to transmit the number 7 to their classmates. The four students will have to determine between them who holds up a 0 and who holds up a 1. The binary sequence for 7 is 0111. The remainder of the students should try to decode the binary number. With more students in the row, higher numbers can be transmitted.

• Have students transmit other scientific data with binary numbers. For example, students can measure the temperature of a liquid or the mass of an object and transmit the results to another student.

• How are binary numbers used in computers?

• How high can you count with a binary number consisting of 10 bits? 12?

ACTIVITY:

Paint by the Numbers Description:

A pencil and paper activity demonstrates how astronomical spacecraft and computers create images of objects in space.

Objective:

To simulate how light collected from a space object converts into binary data and reconverts into an image of the object.

National Education Standards:

Mathematics

Number & operation Patterns, function, & algebra

Measurement

Data analysis, statistics, & probability

Communication

Connections

Representations

Science

Evidence, models, & explanation

Change, constancy, & measurement

Earth in the solar system

Abilities of technological design

Technology

Understand cultural, social, economic, & political effects of technology

Ability to use & maintain technological products & systems

Understand, select, & use:

Medical technologies

Agricultural technologies & biotechnologies

Energy & power technologies

Information & communication technologies

Transportation technologies

Manufacturing technologies

Construction technologies

Materials: (per group of two students)

Transparent grid

Paper grid

Picture of house

Pencil

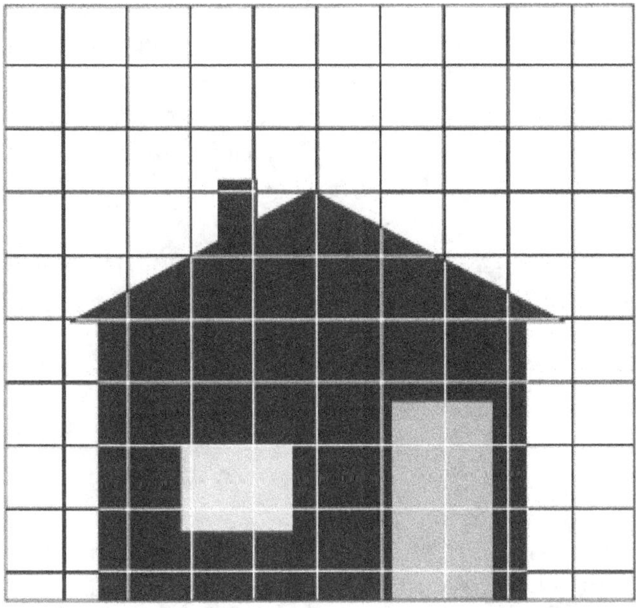

Procedure:

  1. Divide students into pairs.

2. Give one student (A) in each pair the paper copy of the blank grid on the next page. Give the other student (B) in each pair the picture of the house on the next page. Instruct student B not to reveal the picture to student A. Also give student B a copy of the transparent grid. (See notes about making student copies of the picture and grids on the next page.)

3. Explain that the picture is an object being observed at a great distance. It will be scanned by an optical device like those found on some astronomical satellites and an image will be created on the paper.

4. Have student B place the grid over the picture. Student B should look at the brightness of each square defined by the grid lines and assign it a number according to the chart above the picture. Student

B will then call out the number to student A. If a particular square covers an area of the picture that is both light and dark, student B should estimate its average brightness and assign an intermediate value to the square such as a 1 or a 2.

Note: The letters and numbers on two sides of the grid can assist the receiving student in finding the location of each square to be shaded.

5. After receiving a number from student B, student A will shade the corresponding square on the grid. If the number is 0, the square should be shaded black. If it is 3, the square should be left as it is.

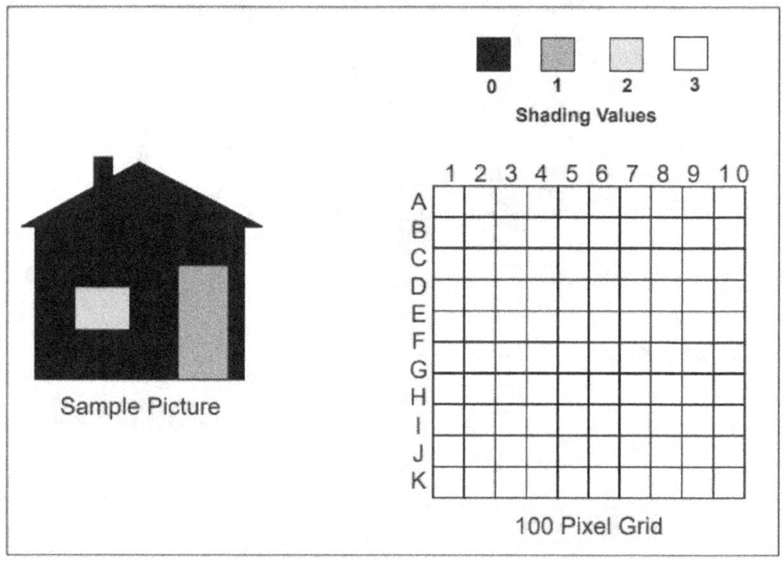

6. Compare the original picture with the image sketched on the paper.

Background:

This activity simulates the process by which an astronomy spacecraft such as the Hubble Space Telescope collects light from an astronomical object and converts the light into a digital form that can be displayed on Earth as an image of the object. The student with the transparent grid represents the spacecraft. The picture is the object the spacecraft is trying to collect from. The student with the paper grid represents the radio receiver on the ground and the image-processing computer that will assemble the image of the object.

The image created with this activity is a crude representation of the original picture. The reason for this is that the initial grid contains only 64 squares (8 x 8). If there were many more squares, each square would be smaller and the image would show finer detail. You may wish to repeat this activity with a grid consisting of 256 squares (16 x 16). However, increasing the number of squares will require more class time.

If you wish to do so, you can select a single student to represent the spacecraft and transmit the data to the rest of the class. With the HST, the grid consists of more than 2.5 million pixels and they are shaded in 256 steps from black to white instead of just the 4 shades used here. Color images of an object are created by the HST with color filters. The spacecraft observes the object through a red filter, a blue filter, and then a green one. Each filter creates a separate image, containing different information. These images are then colored and combined in a process similar to color separations used for printing colored magazine pictures.

Management and Tips:

Students can provide their own pictures for this activity. It is important for the pictures to show strong contrast. The smaller the grid squares, the more detail that will appear in the image. However, simply going from a grid of 10 x 10 to a grid of 20 x 20 will quadruple the length of time it takes to complete the image. Refer to the Color Recognition and Colored Shadows activities for more details on how color filters work and how to combine colors. Assessment: Collect the pictures of the house drawn by the student receivers. Compare the original drawing with the student images. Discuss with your students possible strategies for improving the detail of the images.

Extensions:

· Transmit and reconstruct the image of Saturn shown on the next page. This more advanced picture uses six shades and smaller grid squares.

· Examine printed copies of drawings made with a computer art program. Notice how the pictures are constructed of individual points. Also notice how the size of the points contributes to the fineness of detail in the picture.

· Examine pictures drawn on a computer. Use the magnifying tool to move to the maximum magnification possible. Compare the two views.

· Obtain Hubble Space Telescope images from the Internet sites given in Unit 5. Examine them closely for the pixel structure. Alternately enlarge and reduce the image size on your computer screen to see the effect on the fineness of detail.

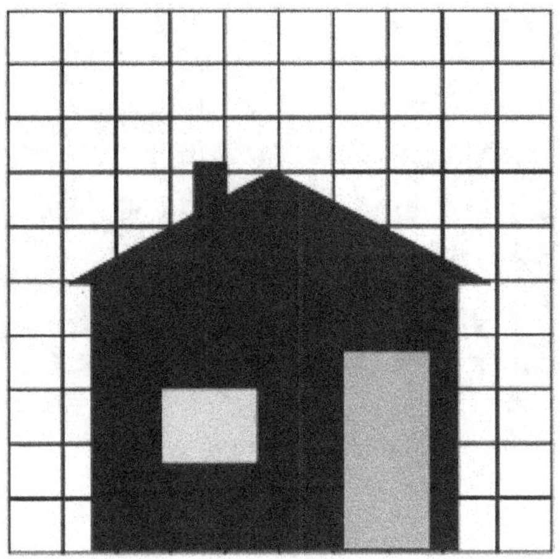

100 Pixel Grid Over House

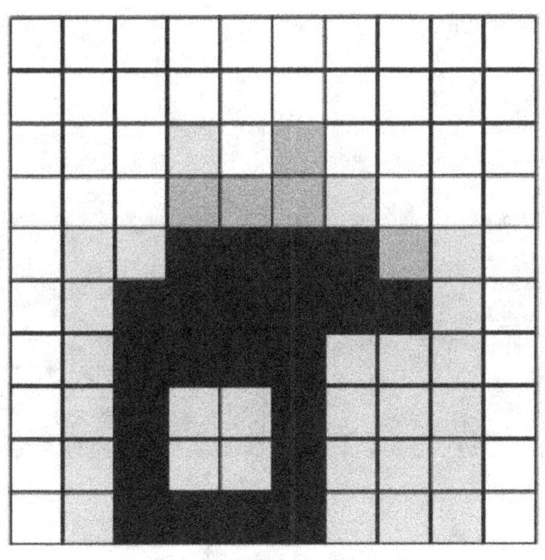

100 Pixel Grid

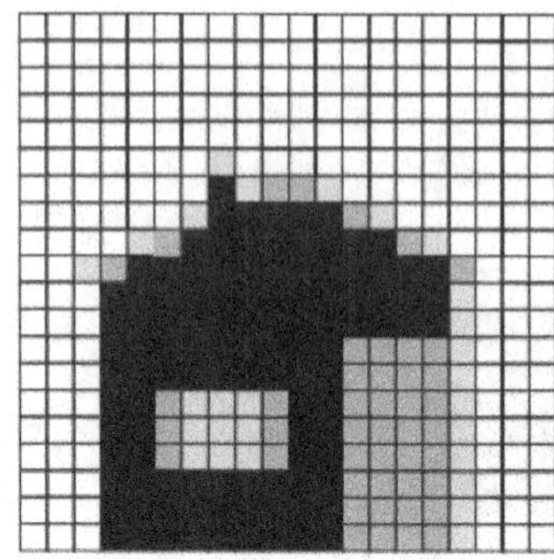

400 Pixel Grid

1,600 Pixel Grid

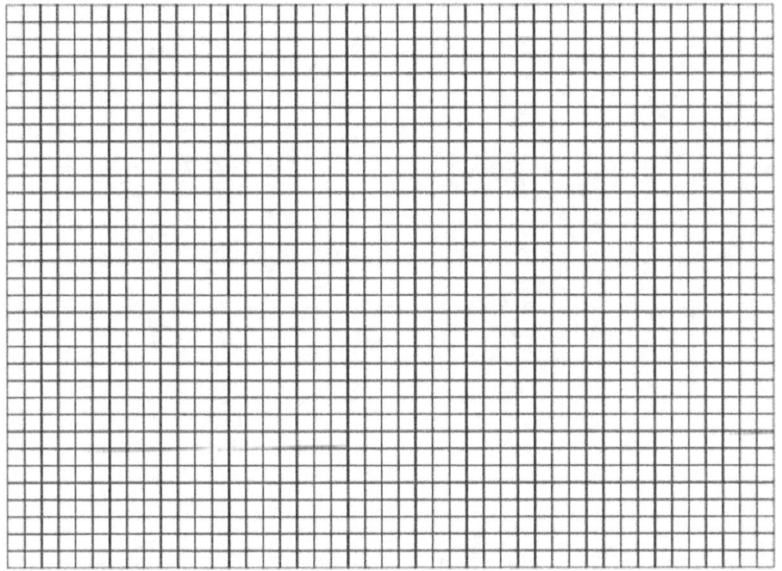